ASPIRE AS MY GRANDMA WOULD SAY

Effective ways to exceed from the wisdom of your legends

ANDREW CM MILLER

WOW Book Publishing™

First Edition Published by Andrew CM Miller

Copyright ©2020 Andrew CM Miller

WOW Book Publishing™

All rights reserved. Neither this book, nor any parts within it may be sold or reproduced in any form without permission.

No part of this book may be reproduced in any form or by any electronic or mechanical means including information storage and retrieval systems, without permission in writing from the author. The only exception is by a reviewer, who may quote short excerpts in a review.

The purpose of this book is to educate and entertain. The views and opinions expressed in this book are that of the author based on his personal experiences and education. The author does not guarantee that anyone following the techniques, suggestions, ideas or strategies will become successful.

The author shall neither be liable nor responsible for any loss or damage allegedly arising from any information or suggestion in this book.

DEDICATION

I wrote this book so that you can identify and rediscover the wisdom given to you from the elderly and other legends that have influenced your life in some way.

I dedicate this book to you as you have now made the exquisite decision to aspire for excellence. As you have committed to your new journey, I am pleased to help you get there.

Peace and Love,

Andrew CM Miller
Your Coach & Author

CONTENTS

Testimonials ix
About the Author xi
Foreword xiii
Acknowledgements xv
Note to the Reader xvii
How To Get The Maximum Benefit From This Book xix

Chapter One
Why Grandma Is Legendary 3
    My Relationship With My Grandma 3
    What My Grandma Says 4
    My Grandma's Traditions 6
    What I Learned From Grandma 9
    How I Learned From My Grandma 10
    The Legacy Of My Grandma 13
    Why My Grandma Was Filled With Wisdom 15
    Grandma's Wealth 16

Chapter Two
Your Legends As Mentors 23
    Who Are Your Legends? 23
    Who Is Your Mentor? 25

Why You Should Have A Mentor 28
Your Mentoring System 30
Your Legend As A Coach... 33
Let Your Legends Lead You 35
The Legacy Of Your Leader 36
What Is Your Legacy?.. 39

Chapter Three
Wisdom From Elders.. 45
Where To Find Wisdom 45
What Is Wisdom?.. 46
Can Wisdom Be Inherited.. 48
How To Gain Wisdom 50
Which Wise Elderly Person Should You Choose?.................... 51
The Wise Grandma... 53
Grandma's Wise Sayings 54
My Wise Learning Curve.. 56

Chapter Four
Successful Pathways 63
Pathways To Success 63
My Success Journeys... 65
Which Path To Take 67
When To Part Ways 68
Success Thinking.. 70
The Right Attitude For Success 71
Your Main Resources.. 73
What If I Choose Another Path? 74

Contents

Chapter Five

Wealth Creation Habits 81
    Wealthy Thinking 81
    Why Have Habits? 83
    What Is Wealth? 84
    Where To Create Wealth 86
    Where To Find Wealth 88
    The Creation Of Habits 90
    What Wealthy People Do 92
    Making And Breaking A Habit 94

Chapter Six

Rich Thinking Attitudes 101
    The Right Attitudes 101
    Richer Thinking 103
    The Rich Ways To Health 105
    Healthy Thinking 106
    Wealthy Thinking 108
    Why Do The Rich Think Big? 109
    Branding Your Views 111
    Thinking Big 113

Chapter Seven

Spirituality And Riches 119
    Spiritual Thinking 119
    The Rich Mentality 120
    Are Rich People Spiritual? 122
    Meditative Approach 123
    Rich Spiritual Habits 125

Meditation And Riches 127
Meditation And Mindfulness 128
Money And Spirituality 130

Chapter Eight
Aspiring To Exceed 137
  My Aspirations To Exceed 137
  Aspire To Achieve 139
  Exceed Your Knowledge Base 141
  How To Exceed Expectations 142
  Aspirations Of My Grandma 144
  Exceed In Wisdom 145
  Aspire To Be Successful 146
  Exceed Your Thinking 148

TESTIMONIALS

"I will advise any parent or carer in a family setting that has relationship issues that they need to read this book: Aspire As My Grandma Would Say."

—Lucina Simmons
Societal Secretary
Kingstown, SVG, W.I.

"Andrew has found a way to connect the wisdom of legends with his own lessons from his elders. 'Aspire As My Grandma Would Say' will act to remind you of the importance of how valuable older folks are in our lives."

—Stanza Nicholas
Senior Civil Servant
London, UK

"For families struggling or wanting to rekindle their joy and purpose, Andrew addresses. 'Aspire As My Grandma Would Say' will highlight key areas that may be lacking."

—Anne T. Miller
Banker
Kingstown, SVG, W.I.

Aspire As My Grandma Would Say

"So many people focus on the things that are happening around them. They forget that all they need maybe within them and they only need to access it. Throughout generations my mother believed & instilled in me that you 'aspire with God and through God.' Andrew will help you identify key components in his book, 'Aspire As My Grandma Would Say.'"

—Jocelyn Sheppard
Retired staff nurse
Canouan Island, St Vincent, W. I.

"Andrew CM Miller has provided you with detailed instructions in order to develop and improve your understanding in relationships with parents, carers and elders. 'Aspire As My Grandma Would Say' contributes to our knowledge by exploring and responding to fundamental questions based on research from our history, culture, race, background and ancestry."

—Nathalie Lynch
Specialist SEN Teaching Assistant | Youth Counsellor
London, UK

"Andrew CM Miller's latest book 'ASPIRE AS MY GRANDMA WOULD SAY' facilitates a means to delve into our relationships with not only our parents but elders as a whole. It provides the opportunity to explore these key relationships and answer those important burning questions of what we have learnt and continue to learn from our past generations. A book worth reading to explore your very own personal experiences"

—Racquel Marter
RN Petit Officer| Specialist Commonwealth mentor
Gosport, UK

ABOUT THE AUTHOR

Andrew CM Miller is an award winning author and coach who continues to inspire and empower individuals to reflect on their life journey and identify what holds them back from taking action. He wrote this book to help you aspire to a higher level of excellence, no matter what.

Andrew has had a range of training and experiences, internationally; both as a student and explored working in various sectors. He worked within the Education, Social Care, and Health Care industries and has been an army reserve soldier for over ten years. Andrew has transformed himself as an award-winning author, and an expert 'transitional coach.'

He develops continuously through leadership training, daily personal development and guidance gained in mentoring and coaching. Andrew's expanded knowledge base, skills-set and education rooted from the Caribbean Islands and branched off as he migrated to the USA; and later settling in the United Kingdom. His discipline then sharpened during his military training and experiences and other personal commitments.

Andrew's hunger for making a difference in people's lives evolved as he aligned himself with elite professionals. This in turn allowed him to challenge his personal mindset. He then re-focused

Aspire As My Grandma Would Say

his efforts, finding his way back to his interest in helping people achieve their dreams and aspirations and reach their true potential.

You can learn more about Andrew on his platforms and at:

www.asmygrandmawouldsay.com

FOREWORD

Dear Reader,

Aspire as My Grandma Would Say is the book to read to help you honour the wisdom of the elderly and the legends of your life who have inspired you.

Andrew has acquired a wealth of mentoring and life coaching skills through the guidance of his legends. He identifies it as 'wisdom' from those who allow him to impart life techniques that you can put into action immediately.

The contents in this book can be used as a guide to your personal success. I can identify with this book as Andrew has awakened within my mind a world of powerful masterminding resources.

Vishal Morjaria
Award-Winning Author
and International Speaker

ACKNOWLEDGEMENTS

Aspirations are built on hope and are associated with actions. To my elders, my grandmothers, my mothers and all my legends, I thank you for the wealth of wisdom you imparted on me.

To my wife and children – you have been without me at different times while I take this journey, especially when I was physically present yet spiritually absent. Thank you for your unimaginable support.

To Ella Williams-Miller, your smile has changed my world. This book is now part of my legacy to you. I acknowledge the nurses, carers, medical, and health staff who have all provided your much needed care.

I acknowledge my extended family, especially my uncle Hyacinth who believed in me and said yes to my adventurous aspirations into the international communities.

I wish to express my appreciation and gratitude to all the people whom I have met along my journey. This book is a tribute to you.

My gratitude goes out to all my support networks: 'The Knowledge Cube—'circle of influence' and especially my 'WOW' and Rockstar connections. To the Big Business Events family and 'The Knowledge Cube CO.' your joint efforts continue to support and develop me into the leader I aspire to be.

Aspire As My Grandma Would Say

I acknowledge the continued influence and works of the Napoleon Hill foundation; John Maxwell, Jim Rhon, Earl Nightingale, Les Brown, Simon Sinek Tony & Nicki Vee and all my discovering legends.

Finally, I acknowledge you for taking the time to invest in yourself. I thank you for taking action today and for receiving and using this book to add value to your life. Now it is your turn.

NOTE TO THE READER

The information, including concepts, opinions, and instructions it contains is based on the author's personal experiences and views and is not intended to provide exclusive professional advice.

The author and the publisher make no warranties, expressed or implied, relating to accuracy, applicability, effectiveness, reliability, or suitability of the contents.

If you wish to apply or follow the advice or recommendations mentioned herein, you take full responsibility for your actions.

The author and publisher of this book shall in no event be held liable for any direct, indirect, incidental, or consequential damages arising from the use of any of the information contained in this book.

All content is for information only and is not warranted for content accuracy or any other implied or explicit purpose.

HOW TO GET THE MAXIMUM BENEFIT FROM THIS BOOK

What do you consider the most important aspect of your life?

Think about this for a moment. What are your thoughts?

Did you think about your mental health? What about your emotions and having a healthy mindset? Did you consider your physical health?

This vital area of your life may surprise you. I have it ingrained within me and I believe you do too. I have tried to disguise or ignore it at times. I knew it and I lived it. How about you?

The three areas of your life: your mental, emotional and physical health are all crucial aspects to maintain. I actually spoke about these in my book: 'The Knowledge Cube Concept'

However, to learn more about this vital area of your life, please read on with an open mind. Thank you!

"Do not waste your time listening to people who are trying to distract you"
—Granny

www.asmygrandmawouldsay.com

CHAPTER ONE
WHY GRANDMA IS LEGENDARY

MY RELATIONSHIP WITH MY GRANDMA

As a child growing up, I would often visit my grandma on school holidays. These visits started when I was an infant. At times, it was as if I was deliberately left behind on Canouan Island while my other siblings and relatives were returning home to the mainland, St Vincent. And so, during these periods, when I stayed with my grandma for so long, if felt like I had been living with her.

These memorable experiences continued into ongoing school holidays. I became more observant and recognised the relationship that was building with my grandma. I was learning her ways, observing her humbleness, and learning from her wisdom.

School holidays with my grandma were almost regimental style settings. Although we had fun, there were things you had to do and things you had to learn. There were chickens to look after, eggs to go and collect, animals to take out, as well as cleaning and tidying around the yard, and at her home. As a reward, I often had that privilege to enjoy the sandy beaches.

Aspire As My Grandma Would Say

I grew to learn that whatever my grandma said, it had a tendency to come to pass. This evolved into my sense of maturity and growth and stayed with me into my adult years. I would remember 'sayings' or thoughts that my grandma said as they just pop up in my mind. And so, in times of trouble, my grandma was sort of there for me. She was often the best point of contact to speak to me, humble me, and teach me a lesson.

She taught me what love was all about, what it entailed, and what to look for. And this was further proven as I developed my relationship with my dad. He too would sometimes ask me questions such as, "What is love? Are you talking about love, or are you talking about feelings? And can you really understand love?"

In my adult years, I still remember what my grandma used to say to me. As I continue to develop my leadership skills, I keep learning from other successful and influential people and keep track of inspirational, life-changing events, organisations, and groups. I am often reminded of grandma's wisdom. And today I can truly acknowledge that my grandma was legendary.

WHAT MY GRANDMA SAYS

As my grandma would say, "Life is short, live it to the fullest" and "Who laughs last, laughs the best." These little sayings have instilled in me certain values, and foundations that I can't simply forget. Today, as I continue my journey into personal development, coaching and mentoring, I still hear 'sayings' like these coming from other leaders, mentors, and successful people.

Today I'm being taught and reminded to focus. As my grandma would say, "Focus on one thing until it's done and that way, you won't have many unfinished things." My grandma, Ella, as she was often called was a very influential woman. She's done many good deeds for people in the community. She helped change and impact their lives in no small way.

As a child growing up, I remember when I attempted to call my grandmother by a name that only adults would call her. It was her first name. I never forgot the harsh look she gave me and the stern tone of voice. She reminded me never to make that mistake again. She insisted that age is not just a number in an adult's life, but a sum of experiences and wisdom that a child should respect. She emphasised on having 'self-respect' and 'respect for the elderly', as well as not interrupt while someone was speaking.

Prayer was a compelling part of our lives as children when we were with our grandma. "It is a powerful thing," she would say. I learned just how powerful that was, especially from my grandma. My grandma was like a visionary in the sense where she would see things before it happened. If she did say something was going to happen, 'it was bound to happen.'

If she said it would rain today, it was going to be raining. She didn't have a meteorologist to tell her what the weather was going to be like. She didn't have weather maps, and she didn't have all those lovely monitoring systems we have. As a child growing up, my grandmother simply looked outside, looked in the sky, looked around, and she was able to tell you what the weather was going to be like for that day. And she was more than 99% correct. And that 1% was only as a result of us falling asleep before that weather condition changed.

My grandma was filled with faith. At times you would ask her what we were going to have for a meal. You may not see her cooking or even preparing a meal. You wouldn't think that there was going to be food available to eat. But at some point, you'll be called for your dinner, and the food would be ready.

My grandma had it all covered. She always reminded me that, "if you don't have salt on your table, you're not managing your home properly." This saying has stayed with me. I sometimes remind my mom about it. Now it's like a 'mantra' in my family and an important house managing tool. I take this same 'saying,' as my grandma would say: "If you don't have salt, you're not managing your home properly."

Grandma's faith was in God, and she would say that she trusted God, not man. Whatever she believed in, she stuck with it; she stuck to her guns. Every decision she made was hers alone, and everyone respected that. She was renowned and known for whatever she said. The older people respected her and us. As children growing up, we respected her. She grew to be a sort of icon in our community. In that little home island: Canouan, where I partly lived.

MY GRANDMA'S TRADITIONS

On reflection, I can recall now how, as a youngster, I discovered that I did not dare stay in bed for a 'lie-in'. As soon as the sun was shining early in the morning, I had to be out of bed. If the sun was up, I was up and out of bed as well. It was a ritual and a norm. This was my grandmother's way, and I didn't try changing it. Of course, I did try challenging this ritual as a youngster growing up, but it didn't really matter. It was just the way it was, and it was my grandma's rule.

To an extent, I have kept this practice with me, just as my grandma says: As the sun is up, I ought to be awake and up out of bed. As such, you may not see me sleeping during the day. Early rising, as my grandma instilled in me, is something I hear more often today. Similarly, I have heard it repeatedly from the great motivational leader and speaker, Les Brown. He insists that, "Get up early in the morning and start the day at least an hour before everyone (you) normally gets up."

Starting earlier than the norm usual gives you a level of natural energy. This early start will allow you to plan and prepare for the rest of the day and propels you forward with that extra force. Other leaders, including the inspirational Earl Nightingale and the teachings of Napoleon Hill (Think & Grow Rich), have both shared similar thoughts around getting up early and starting your day before you usually do.

My grandma's traditions included prayer and meditation. Every morning as she got up, she would be on her knees. Later she adopted a dedicated location in her 'special chair' as her knees weakened. Her rising early did not waiver. Whether in ill health or not, she would pray. Well, I smile now as I am not sure what the other choices were. My grandma's praying became a family practice.

School holidays, especially when there was a group of us staying with my grandma, we'd join her in prayer. This instilled within me a higher value of moral and ethics. This has helped me to grow with a better sense of judgement and a better understanding of right and wrong. Later in life, I've learned a lot of self-control, especially as I continue to learn the importance and power of meditation and visualisation.

My grandma was often happy to have tea ready for me in the morning. However, she seemed always to have her lovely, infused drink of coffee. I would always rush to try to get half a cup. And at times I'd be challenged by my cousins. We had this sense of clinging toward our grandma. Perhaps it was the wealth of wisdom which she carried or just her love, her warmth and her care for us.

Aspire As My Grandma Would Say

On my weekend visits, grandma would urge my other siblings and me to go to church. Her view was that we should acknowledge Sunday as the Lord's Day. Grandma would go on to say that (we) I should take some time of the seven days of the week to pay our respect and take rests. Her view was that you should change the programme, that is generally acceptable. You should not live each day always in 'such a rush,' on the go.

Grandma insisted that at some point, you should stop! That you should listen to the silence around you. Put some time aside so that you can, pray, meditate, and feel renewed. My grandma emphasised on the importance of reflection, so you can feel the effects and grow from your experiences. This was a significant part of the journey with my grandma and her instilling values in me as a young man. So, I share this with you today. You can add value to your journey and growth.

My grandma's traditions continue to stay with me today. Many of these traditional practices and values seem to be reappearing in my life. In fact, several of my mentors, and personal life coaches who continue to help guide my life's journey, also share grandma's values with me today. They too have claimed that an early rise, and an early start of the day, makes the day more productive and more successful. And so, my grandma's tradition "lives on" and continues with me today.

I wish to challenge you today—consider the way you start your day. What practices or inclinations do you have? What daily rituals do you follow? Why not 'Aspire;' As My Grandma would say: start the day early, and include an element of meditation, each day.

Why Grandma Is Legendary

WHAT I LEARNED FROM GRANDMA

As mentioned earlier, my grandma's love was with her higher power. I knew very little about her relationship with her husband 'Daddy Mac,' my grandfather. As I would learn later, my grandmother was like an iron-woman and mother. She was a pivot point in many of our lives, in our community, and our family. My grandma taught me how to love. She taught me what love is, what it looked like, what it can feel like. A lot of it I had to experience for myself, but she indicated to me those key areas that I needed to know.

Love is powerful. Later, as I experienced and learned, love is kind and gentle. Love can sometimes be perceived as dangerous. Love is a decision that we can take, and it's a journey. Love can be many things. But my grandma's love in her higher power was something more profound.

Grandma's influence on love helped to instil in me my own belief systems. It has helped me shape and reform the root of my beliefs and how I visualise my own life journey. This much to the point where my humbleness has grown out of my own beliefs and systems. Morality was a big part of my grandma's way of life. And as my grandma would say, "the only fear you should have is the 'fear of God'."

There were times when I felt safe, fearless, and at times, when I felt mightily. And as my grandma would say, remember to be humble. I, too, experienced periods of humbleness in my growth and development and my ethical thinking. And as my grandma would say, "Ethics and values will take us a long way."

So, I believe that I have ethical thinking to a point where I don't believe in simply receiving. I have a keen belief that you must give as well. More importantly, you must not give, only to receive. Instead, this is a natural type of transaction, which you must have.

I have learnt this, and I do insist too that you cannot only think there is just give or receive.

If, and when, you do give, you must be open to receiving. Similarly, when you're receiving, you must be prepared to give. Give of yourself, give of your wealth, your earnings, whatever you choose. Be grateful when receiving, but equally be kind and courteous in your giving.

What I learned from my grandma has brought me to this stage in my life. Many of her values have helped me to grow and to be a stronger person, allowing me to become a robust coach or mentor. I can stand firm and share with you today my own experiences in the hope that you can identify your experiences with your elderly – with your grandmas, your guides, your carers. All the people you consider as your own legends in life.

I encourage you today to respect and value that which has been transferred or passed on to you from the elderly. Take time out to reflect on what you may have learned from your own legends as you carry on your life's journey – this journey of life. Be appreciative of your journey of excellence, your journey to exceed.

HOW I LEARNED FROM MY GRANDMA

As a young man growing up, I did have my share of complicated experiences. As a child, I was somewhat restricted with my mother's parenting styles. My mom was seemingly frustrated most of the time. When I would go to spend time with my grandma or was in her midst, she would allow me to explore. I would often enjoy nature and go to different places with my friends.

In many ways, the early stages of exploring created my interest in nature. I ventured amongst the wildlife. I swam among creatures I had never seen or heard of before. I even scurried through encyclopaedias looking for some of them. I have been around rocks while coasteering and on exclusive beachfronts. I've helped to look after some of my friends' herds of animals. At this early stage of my life, I had this amazing period when I was able to explore with some of my friends and other siblings freely.

As I stretch my hands outward, I can close my eyes with my head pushed back and looking up in the sky I can reminisce. And dancing slowly, as if listening to mellow music, I can imagine the peacefulness. Visiting my grandma did allow me to grow and live freely and naturally.

When in the immediate environment of my grandma, I remember how things appeared. She did seem to be very independent. My grandma was filled with faith and appeared quite self-sufficient. On her property, she had crops growing, and she had several animals. Grandma even had fruit trees growing, even though most of the time, she did not eat from them.

I knew that she was retired, yet she still had people in the community that came out to seek her advice or to seek her healing. I suppose this reflected on the fact that she was a nurse for an extended part of her life. Grandma dedicated herself to serving others and had a strong belief in prayer, meditation, and relaxing in silence. Toward the end of her life, I enjoyed seeing my grandma relaxing, looking over the ocean and reminiscing 'at times gone by.' She had a nice view of a beautiful ocean on the beautiful island of Canouan, St Vincent, in the Caribbean.

Being part of an extended community, I have delved into various childhood experiences, especially with my other siblings and friends. I was able to go fishing and hunting and I would often extend this freedom. I swam a lot in the shallow areas of beaches, and my grandma had a way of being able to 'see beyond.' I don't know how she saw me from such a distance at times. She would warn me when there were sharks or when it would seem unsafe to go on the beaches.

I would laugh at times, and then I would hear the news a few days later, on the radio broadcast, or from within the village community, warning about sharks. I sometimes thought that perhaps grandma knew as there was some crystal-clear skies type of weather. However, and whatever it was, she knew for some reason. My grandma foresaw things or predicted events. I doubted my grandma's wisdom at times, and there were often some rough patches, at the early stages.

I often boarded a vessel—a small fishing boat—called 'The Golden Eagle.' Don't ask me why. I believe it had a way of gliding on the sea. I still don't know for sure. My uncle owned it at some stage; then he didn't. Secretly, I would swim out to the boat, climb aboard and pretend that I was the captain. I would sail the boat like an eagle flying in the sky. I laugh at this idea, even now. At least I was a child with sprouting dreams. Later, my grandma found out, and I still don't know how she did. One view was that she saw me several times.

Later, in my various adventurous quests, I was able to go island hopping, at different times, between the beautiful Grenadine islands. In all this experience, my grandma allowed me to explore and to learn things from nature, my surroundings, my siblings, and my friends.

As I look back on my childhood, sometimes I realise that 'as you grow, you become restricted in your life.' This is often due to our travelling, our going to schools, and growing up quickly. Being under life's pressures, we tend to forget what it's like to be free and dream. My grandma introduced me to Bible reading and her deep and intimate praying.

Why Grandma Is Legendary

As my grandma would say, "The heart of wisdom lies in the scriptures." And so, it took me some time, but with my grandma's advice, I later delved into reading different parts of the Bible. I then started to see older people in my life, particularly the ill in health or the sick and dying, who I learned from as well. I learned from these people, as I continued to read and learn from the scriptures. I learned and gained a wealth of wisdom from those with ill health, the elderly and sick who were, 'bedded down,' just as I did from my grandma.

THE LEGACY OF MY GRANDMA

My grandma was very hard-working. As my grandma would say, "Hard work does pay off." My grandma spoke to me a lot about service to others. And perhaps this is one reason why I led off into my previous and my current journeys into the service industries. This included my actual work in the education sector, in the health and wellness industries, and health and social care services.

I managed to do a bit of travelling to various places, including several islands and countries. These opportunities evolved from most of the volunteer work that I carried out. Additionally, I am very appreciative for my period of service in the British Army. This employment allowed me to have some exciting and interesting periods of exploration, too.

I travelled to the Caribbean Island of Jamaica at one stage, visiting the Missionaries of the Poor. I ventured out on tasks with 'Helping Hands' in Brooklyn, New York. I was also fascinated on a trip to Toronto, Canada, having observed the way that the elderly come out on the weekend for a meal and socialise, eating simply in the malls and fast-food restaurants. In North Lauderdale, Florida, again, I enjoyed the community spirit and engaged in conversations with the elderly. All this reminded me of the legacy of my grandma.

Aspire As My Grandma Would Say

As my grandma mothered the community and environment in which she grew up around, it reminded me how hard she worked. As a retired nurse, my grandma continued to reach out to the heart of the community while at home. My grandma was still being recommended as a professional and as a source of guidance.

I can admit that my grandma was not always the quiet, relaxed, chilled out, angelic lady she appeared to be. It even makes me smile saying this. She had a festivity for drinking, and she encouraged me as well to have my little sips during the celebration periods. At Christmas and especially during Easter, I tended to call myself a festive drinker at one stage. This thought then moved into a seasonal drinker, meaning drinking alcohol and beverages and celebrating at different seasonal activities.

My grandma also told me: "don't be ungrateful!" Learning to give thanks was a big part of growing up. So again, meditation, prayer, and being grateful became common trends. I noticed at Christmas time how Grandma's home always had guests visiting. There always seemed to be an influx of friends and visitors. They moved between and amongst the houses in the communities and nearby villages. Most times, they were given a drink or some cake that my grandma often had prepared.

I particularly enjoyed the drinks, especially the rum punch. And this particular recipe seemed to have been 'passed-down' the generations of my family. I've seen my grandma's drinks being made by my mother and later by my older sister. This sense of legacy drives my inspiration. My grandma's middle name has moved down to several generations within my family.

When I had met several of my grandma's sisters' and several of my grandmother's siblings, they too displayed similar levels and systems of wisdom. I can only imagine how their wealth of learning and spirituality, combined with my grandma, must have created a legacy of legends. The legacy of my grandma will continue to move forward in this book and the communities I work with. In particular, the people I help to inspire, and whose lives I continue to improve. So why not you?

WHY MY GRANDMA WAS FILLED WITH WISDOM

It may seem odd at times, but yes, my grandma was filled with wisdom. Mainly through her simplicity. This included simplicity in the way she lived her life, in the way she served and how she committed to work with people. Every little bit that she did seemed to inspire and seemed to move forces. My grandma seemed to make a change in someone's life, every time.

My grandmother's simplicity came from a spirit of oneness. Her oneness was in the sense of focusing on herself to serve. Some people may even refer to this today as being selfish. She was filled with faith. She embraced her faith in the Bible, faith in herself, and faith in God. And she lived this faith through Sunday worship, daily prayer, and in achieving. She followed through by acting, and through her belief in her inner strength. In a sense, I would say my grandma lived without fear. And as she would say, "The only fear you should have is the fear of God."

My grandma encouraged me not to live with fear. She would look at me and insist on learning to be brave, to commit to being outstanding, and to let my light shine. "Don't be afraid to help others," my grandma would say. 'Do not hesitate to serve others.' And help the less fortunate.

As I write this book, I write to you, saying the same things to you. 'Let fear be.' If it ever enters your life, let it propel you and drive you forward. Do not let fear hold you back. Do not let fear become an unstoppable obstacle in your life. Let fear drive you.

My grandma created healthy atmospheres. She believed in living within healthy environments and in many ways, create it. She tried to keep negative activity away from her, and if it so became present or came to her, she would rebuke it. If something unhealthy or negative became part of my grandmother's environment, she tended to encourage me to get rid of it. As my grandma would say and insist: "think more positively and have more faith." Be sterner and firm, she would say, and be encouraging. All in all, you will live more healthier, and think more positively.

As my grandma would say, "A healthy mind is a healthy you." My grandma was filled with wisdom as she grew in strength day by day and shared in her wisdom.

How about your thoughts on your mental health? What do you think about the most? Is it mostly empowering thoughts?

GRANDMA'S WEALTH

My grandma's wealth came from her general achievements. This was not just monetary wealth. My grandma had lived a comfortable life, and she had served the villages well. She always believed in looking after our community. Many times, I wanted to be in her midst. At times, I'd have to compete as there was always another family member needing her time. My grandma would encourage me to learn to live and be together.

My grandmother worked hard and earned little financially. She did, however, manage to build a house. She loved telling me her stories, too. She left a lot of property behind, when she passed on, and her wealth included different real-estate. But it was the rewards of bringing families together and passing on her wisdom and her values that proved more worthy of wealthiness.

Grandma had certain peculiar values. Some of which she created, and others she gained. When I look back at her tangible property, I realise its value and worth in a commercial sense. Today I can appreciate that she worked hard and that she was rewarded. She gained decent monetary wealth, yet she left it all behind with thanks.

My grandma's house that she retired into overlooked a beautiful ocean. It's one of the most beautiful views I've seen in the world. You can see a wide, beautiful ocean filled with peace and tranquillity and healthiness. It was an environment where you could easily meditate within and feel free. You mostly live in tranquillity.

As I reflect on my grandma sitting in her porch, looking over the balcony sometimes in silence, I have often wondered what she thought about. And as she looked out toward the ocean, sometimes with a smile on her face, I would often imagine her thoughts. Although she did share some of the disappointments in her life, she also shared thoughts of her impactful life.

At times when I asked a question, my grandma's expression didn't change much. It was almost as if she didn't register the question. Her mood would not appear to change in the first instance. It was as if her thought process would not get interrupted.

As I reflect on those times, I take a deeper look around at the livestock on my grandma's lands. I realised that most of the animals were not even owned by her. She just allowed other people's animals to roam as they graze. My grandma would allow other people to use her lands to look after their livestock. They would look after their animals and treat themselves to some of the fruit trees on the property and the surrounding lands.

Aspire As My Grandma Would Say

I can truly say that my grandma's wealth included serving others and giving. Rather than just receiving, my grandma's wealth truly evolved as a result of her service to others, the communities and her family life.

Why Grandma Is Legendary

Notes

"There is a reason why the other man thinks and acts as he does"
—Dale Carnegie

www.asmygrandmawouldsay.com

CHAPTER TWO
YOUR LEGENDS AS MENTORS

WHO ARE YOUR LEGENDS?

My grandma has been, of course, one of my earlier legends and still is. Sometimes, in conversations, I contemplate what I'm about to do. Let's say, a certain thought comes to my mind. That thought or phrase: "as my grandma would say . . . :", appears in my mind. It is almost like a preliminary confirmation to an action. You may have heard similar types of phrases like, "Jack of all trades, master of none."

As I remember some of these 'sayings', I have often thought about the origins. I have concluded that most times an elderly person may have said it. Many times, I think, only my grandma would say 'such a thing' to me. Yet today, as I experience the writings and sayings shared by coaches, I can picture my grandma and sometimes other influential and popular leaders. I hear them all saying similar things. You hear them saying the same things.

My grandma must have been onto something when she continually reminded me, "there is nothing new under the sun." She would say: "Andrew, try to focus. Focus on one thing at a time, focus on getting what you're doing now. And that is when you go onto the next thing." Did I listen? In fact, when my grandma said, "In this way, you're sure to achieve what you're trying to do," I think I switched off. Today, I can say: *Lesson learned.* Yes, after several expensive and challenging years as well.

As I think of what my grandma might say, I would consider the ideas of other 'change leaders' like Henry Ford (1800-1900s). As you walk about and see different technological advancement, he has been one of the main pioneers behind it. You can even drive about in a Ford modelled or branded vehicle. You can look at the history and look at the legacy, too. You can see how someone like Henry Ford was a legend; how he came up with his ideas about automobiles. In fact, he was part of the mastermind generation, sharing similar minds to others who created history. Others who became legends in their communities and who led the evolution of industries.

Today, we can see the word 'Ford' still exists and is labelled and branded on vehicles. This was done over many years and continues to go on today. And the word Ford is akin to brands such as: Rolls Royce, BMW, Mercedes or Toyota. These brands all have their own legacy attached to their initial ideas. These came from people who envisioned something out of the ordinary and out of their comfort zone. I consider them as pioneers, just as Andrew Carnegie who thought of ideas and influenced the entire steel and mining industries.

Andrew Carnegie initiated sets of challenges and set the cornerstone for many of today's industrial advancements, some household appliances, and some machinery still used daily. As you go about your busy moments travelling on trains, and perhaps railways, you may not think of someone like Andrew Carnegie. Yet he has been a true inspiration and contributor to what was started many years ago. He has also been a major influence on other

Your Legends As Mentors

pioneers, such as: Henry Ford, Thomas Edison and other legends you will become familiar with time.

Importantly Dale Carnegie (Carnagey) continues to inspire many people. Today I consider him a true legend. During the period of Andrew Carnegie, another of my legends, Napoleon Hill was being inspired. At the time of writing this, the Napoleon Hill Foundation continues to carry on Hill's work. Many of Hill's writings have inspired and encouraged me to explore several concepts of my masterminding and other various projects.

Napoleon Hill has been a true legend and continues to be another of my legends. His writings and ideas helped give birth to another of my book titles: "The Knowledge Cube Concept—*Ignite Your Passion to Become Successful.*" And his life work continues to inspire many other people. One of his books, 'Think and Grow Rich,' continues to hold a place in my library and it has become a reference book. At times, I revisit his books in some of my work activities, especially his 'Laws of Success' principles.

Napoleon Hill did set out on a truly inspirational journey that relates to the legacy of both Ford and the Carnegies indirectly. My wisdom gained through my grandma sayings has propelled me forward—and I am certain my grandma hasn't read Hill's books. In fact, she surely never mentioned any of these names to me. Today, my grandma continues to be one of my true legends—an influence and a guide.

Why not consider your influences. Who have been your mentors? Who are your legends?

WHO IS YOUR MENTOR?

Throughout my inspirational journeys, I have found myself working with various coaches and mentors. When I mention my mentors to other people, they look at me in a weird way. Some have indicated the impact of others on their learning, and other times I have had questions thrown at me. "How can you possibly not have met some of these people you talk about so much?", or "How could you consider them mentors?"

I often refer to some individuals as my 'secret mentors' because a person may not know who I am, personally, yet influence me regularly. I have shared that through their influences: their writings, through their publications, their audios. Or from speeches, or audio books today. I learn and continue to develop through their teaching, sharing, and training. These 'secret mentors' have become my mentors because they have achieved that which I have been aspiring to. They have already achieved similar success, and wealth.

In achieving my goals and getting through my various tasks, I then look back at some of my previous work and earlier writings of some of my legends. In comparing the work of legends and some leaders, I look at and conclude that this surely works as a guide for me. For anything you do, I believe everyone should have a "secret mentor" or guide.

Perhaps you haven't recognised this just yet. Maybe you don't even want to acknowledge it. Either way, there is someone out there who you may want to emulate. Someone whom you have taken advice from. Or someone whose memorable phrases have influenced you. Perhaps 'as my grandmother would say . . . ' type of idea that has helped guide you. And, 'As my grandma would say,' " look before you leap!" Even simple little things like this, I sometimes remember.

Your grandma (or nan) may not be with you, physically; however, imagine if your grandma, or your legend—your 'secret mentor' was speaking directly to you, right now. That individual would surely have something to share with you that will be influential.

Choosing a mentor is up to you. Selecting who you want to work with, who you want to listen to, or who you want to be guided by, is all up to you. Who do you want to help you to improve your drive to move forward? It's all up to you and your own decision. Your choice as a mentor should be someone who has already achieved some levels of success. Someone who achieved something, especially in line with what you're looking to achieve. You may have an elderly person whom you admired or perhaps someone who impacted your path and your decision-making. They too can be referred to as your mentor.

As I look out upon the horizon today, I see clear blue skies. This reminds me of a holiday view in the sunny Caribbean island, Barbados. It is early in the morning. It's before breakfast and I have just about finished a visualisation period or 'time out.' As I open my eyes, I see the sun rising. At the same time, the birds are chirping loudly, both distantly and near me. The rooster's nearby crow, making its: 'cock-a-doodle-doo' sound, reminding me that it's time!

You may not have the nicest of weathers where you are right now. So, as you read this, why not take that time out to reflect. Dream for a little bit. And as you smile, consider this: 'Who do I want to be guided by?' In fact, whatever or whomever you decide to choose to be inspired by today, always remember that there is some other person, 'in need', later in your life. Perhaps, even right now, there may be someone looking for you to guide them. Someone looking for you to take on a new journey with them, to achieving success.

You too can become a mentor just as you select your own mentor and success coach. Choose your own mentor. Create your own story. You will have a better understanding of what it feels like when you are being 'sought after.' You'll be able to experience the shared value at some point, when you mentor someone else. Inspire someone else. This often has a reciprocal effect. Why not give yourself the chance to see that there is a true area of calling, within you.

Very often, I have found that in order to be mentored, some sort of reward must be involved. As my grandma would say: 'You must give to get.' Even if something is gifted to you, even intangible, such as guidance towards your path in life, you will be expected to give back, at some stage. This is a very important point to note. Either way, there is value in choosing your mentor, today.

WHY YOU SHOULD HAVE A MENTOR

Very often I meet people who struggle with similar issues, and claim: "Oh, I don't have a role model. I don't need a role model." These are components of various things my grandmother inspired me to resolve. As a young man exploring, I have been inspired by older people and other people in my 'circle of influence' that I often interacted with. They have all encouraged me to be open-minded to learning and being guided by my ancestors. With this, I developed the inspiration to seek wisdom and aspire to become more of what I am as I learn from experiences with my grandma.

Having goals, having intentions and having what I consider ambition need some form of forward thinking. From what I learned from my grandmother, being guided should be in different ways, whether directly or indirectly. I have considered the need to be mentored in almost everything I do. Everything I want to achieve and in any aspect of life, I tend to look for a leader in that industry, or in that profession. Someone on that path who can guide me, who I can follow my desire to explore and venture out.

Your Legends As Mentors

You get guidance or help that way, be it directly or indirectly. I believe that you must have willingness to venture first, even though mentoring is very important. You must be guided by something or by someone. At some stage in your life, I suggest that you connect with someone who has possibly achieved close to or exactly what you want to achieve now. I insist on the 'close to.'

Your mentor could take various forms. You could have a silent mentor as I've mentioned before. You could select mentors through audio tapes, or through attending workshops and training. You may select to pay for a mentor straight away. It always comes down to what you're looking to achieve and how soon or in what way you want to achieve it.

Over some time, I have introduced, tested and implemented the idea of buddy mentoring. Buddy mentoring is where you have a 'chummy relation' with someone who is going to be more of an accountability partner and not simply a supportive friend. In this way you are not going to be engaged in routine chattering or having a good laugh. Instead, choose someone who is interested in your own aspirations, and both of you would support each other's set goals. This may be monthly targets, tasks for each week or daily activities. Either way, you set aside a few hours to follow up with each other.

You can decide when you want to speak and how long you want to speak for. As a matter of accountability, be open and share everything with each other, and if you need help, ask for it. Where you may need some guidance, find ways on how best you can support each other. You can reach out to me for more in-depth guidance on this method of mentoring. There are profound individual rewards from doing this correctly.

The fact that you're reading this book and reading this chapter right now tells me that I may be able to extend some degree of support and mentoring to you. Perhaps one of my team members may be able to assist you, so feel free to reach out. The contact information is provided in this book. I would love to know more about your experience. Whichever way you choose, I do hope you find support that will help you decide why you should have a mentor.

I have accessed my grandma's memories frequently, as a mentoring guide. Her memories would not be enough to carry me along every time. Sometimes, when I really feel like I'm down in a rut and I need someone to lift me up, I access that link with my buddy. I recall one of my earlier mentors saying, "Andrew, when you're feeling up, reach down. When you're feeling down, reach up (for help)." It is precisely for this reason why you have a mentor that you could reach up to. Someone that can help pull you up and help pull you out when you need it.

Your mentor will be someone who triggers your motivation. Whether you are having that negative feeling or if you're already upward in your drive, they will be there to further assist and help propel you and move you forward more quickly. Your mentor is that guidance moving you forward in achieving what you want. They can assist you in achieving your goals and help you explore possibilities in order to become a better you.

I am aware that the most successful people I know, if not all, have mentors. In fact, I believe that even those I don't know have mentors, too. Have you considered why you should have a mentor? Read this chapter again if you need to and learn why it is essential to have a guide in your journey to success.

YOUR MENTORING SYSTEM

I have mentioned before that your mentoring system could result in something like a guide. It may be a set of workshop trainings you attend routinely. And this should be by someone who is qualified, someone who is ahead of you in your own game too. You can choose a 'buddy up' system in a way that works for you. Do this if you are working with peers that have similar goals. You may find others in a similar physical location that you are able to interact with on the same level, particularly according to their needs.

Do you have someone who could be your accountability partner? Someone who's reliable and is playing the game, your game? Do you have someone who wants to work with you and is helping themselves to propel forward with you? Someone who is helping you move along in the right direction? Why not consider setting up and reviewing your 'buddy up' system, today?

Your mentoring system needs to be personalised to you, regardless whether you decide to work with someone exclusive to your industry or someone external of your physical location. Always keep records of what you're doing. This is another form of accountability and it helps to track your progress. Keep records of what you're doing, consistently. When you interact with your mentor directly or indirectly, keep your records. This in turn will help you create your own mentoring system and help keep track of what you're doing. And it is one of the easiest ways to stay true to your purpose and goals.

Keeping records will allow you to make changes while you are being guided by what you're doing. The records will also help to guide you with your finances, whether you are investing in yourself or within your budgeting system. Your own records will help in goal setting and creating tasks, while keeping your finances on track. Whenever you achieve a task or a goal, why not celebrate? You should celebrate your progress when you stick to your routine of monitoring and keeping a record of what you're doing along with your successes.

Aspire As My Grandma Would Say

Even though all this is optional, consider the benefits for a second. When you keep track of what you're doing, you feel a certain fulfilment. As you continue to tick off different tasks, you feel motivated to carry on. As you achieve your goals along the way, you can reward yourself. It is imperative though to have a system as there is no use just doing everything and going everywhere senselessly. Work along your list and create your system.

Imagine for a moment that you have five items in your system or on your list, right now. As you are going through the first one, you may be halfway or three quarters of the way finished, but you touch on the next one and the next one because you're not monitoring your progress. That is because your mini-successes and what you're achieving right now is not being monitored correctly. If that's the case, you may tend to restart at different times.

What if instead, you had started with number one and you tick it off when you achieve it, and then you do number two and three and so on, and tick (check) it along the way. At the end of the process you would have achieved all your tasks. When it's all said and done, you can now have a celebratory period. Whether it's a glass of wine, a non-alcoholic beverage, going to a film, watch a movie, or however you choose to celebrate. Monitor your successes. Keep track of your tasks and you will achieve them, continuously.

This is where accountability comes into play. First, be accountable to yourself. Yes! And be accountable as you pursue and achieve your tasks. Be accountable as you tick the check boxes. This will give you time to check, reflect and reconsider or adjust what you're doing.

Once you are on track or even if you are distracted, you can become aware where or how you got derailed. By being accountable, you can refocus and get back on your journey. As you continue to follow your system and focus in, you will appreciate the reliability and effectiveness of your mentoring style system. Follow the advice given to you by your mentor, coach or confidant. Have a system and follow it as you see fit and as it relates to your progress and success.

YOUR LEGEND AS A COACH

Earl Nightingale can surely be seen as one of my legends and coaches. I would say Earl Nightingale is truly a legend in his publications and audio recordings. I have been able to journey through some of his works, and they guide me on a daily basis. His works have pioneered in the area of personal development and the life transformation industry.

I have been studying Earl's writings, his articles and listening to his audio tapes. I can truly say that they share my world philosophy, my visions and some of my success avenues. While examining Earl Nightingale's many years of work, I have come to the conclusion that in choosing your coach there are many things you can explore. Earl Nightingale was an advocate for, as my grandmother would say: a noble attitude (high moral principles). He also shared the idea of having the right attitude about systems and similar laws. Particularly, laws of success.

Choosing your coach is always up to you. You must be comfortable with who you're working with and what you're doing. As my grandmother would say: "listen before you speak." Listening is very often one of the most effective ways to learn. My experience with the whole idea of listening and silence has been profound. When you're silent, you can listen even more clearly.

My grandma's 'sayings' continue to help coach me into who I am becoming. Her influences have been shaping my moral aspects and my ethics. I can truly say that many of the thoughts and guidance from my grandma are more of what I see in a legendary coach.

My grandma was accessible, and I was willing. I have been taught by other leaders in various industries and continue to learn from other coaches. One thing has been common: 'You must become coachable, in order to be coached'.

When my grandmother spoke, I listened! Very often, whatever my grandma said, it was not debatable. I also had the opportunity to verify it as definitely correct. If it was not correct today, then sometime in the future, it would be. At times my grandma would challenge me. "You may not understand now," she would say, "but your time will come." And as my grandma would say, my time did come to experience and acknowledge that manifestation.

My time truly came. It was realised while I write this book in addition to similar times when I set out on several adventures of my life's journeys. And my 'time came' again while the idea of having a coach popped into my mind. And as my grandma would say: "You're never too old to learn."

My grandma reminded me that as I attend, say tertiary education or high-level learning, I should never lose respect for parents or guardians. And, she would go on to say: "never tell yourselves that you know too much." And that I can grow and learn at any stage in my life. She insisted that I make learning, 'a continuous thing'. My grandma may not have seemed the most educated person, but my life was filled with journeys and experiences from her wisdom. I can truly call her a legend and my coach.

I share and identify with you, some of what I have learnt in my life as influenced by older people in my life. I have also used this wisdom to support other people on their journey.

Now it is your turn. Who are your legends? Who do you have that has had an influence in your life, that you consider an earlier coach?

LET YOUR LEGENDS LEAD YOU

Those before us, including our ancestors, have been through their journeys. They have been through life experiences that you and I don't need to try and relive, all over again. They have set a pathway. My grandma's sayings have been pointers in life. You might remember different stages, especially when something may have occurred, and you need a reminder in your life. While on your journey you will need to identify when to take the next turn or start a new path.

My grandma's sayings came from the elders' journeys. You may think today that you are living in a brand-new time or in a new arena. But as you know, life is an ongoing journey, with many ups and downs. And it goes around and comes back around.

Grandma has been a true inspiration for me. There are many things that she's helped me identify in my life. Some of these inspirational episodes include some of what I have already experienced, and of what I perceive to encounter as challenges. At this stage, I have either experienced many of them already or I am experiencing many of them currently, as part of my journey. My grandma's inspiration continues to help me through my current stages in my life. Her guidance has helped bring me to this point in my life where I feel I can 'lift off' whenever I choose to, using a combination of her wisdom and that of other legends.

Many times, I feel that I have a clear picture of what to expect on my journeys. I believe that you too can have this feeling. I have had the privilege of visiting several countries and their different environments. This has increased my networking with different people. From this network of people, I have had the privilege to learn from their own experiences, life journeys, knowledge and their skills.

Aspire As My Grandma Would Say

What about you? What about your own experiences? This is training. In fact, it can be ongoing training if you show willingness and dedication.

I can truly say that your network of people gives you a wealth of experience to build on. It may be from your peers who join you in your journey. It may be some new ideas that have come from other people. This may include industrial leaders, be it in music, entertainment, education or in your health. Some of the people you meet and network with have already been through many of these experiences. They have had different life journeys and you too can learn from them.

Industrial leaders have not only created industries. Some of them have pioneered what you would call today 'branding'. From what started long ago and years upon years of research behind them, they all put in their individual efforts. Which is why their knowledge and experiences are available today. You can truly say and identify your leaders who have led the way. Why not let your leaders or legends lead you today?

THE LEGACY OF YOUR LEADER

I believe that the way our lives are today is greatly influenced by past experiences. What we do today is just walking down the proverbial path of past legends. Today, you may think that you are living your own experiences. Yet, what you and I may think is new to us, it is only the result of what others have already created. They have provided a blueprint for us to use.

I have observed how artists like Kanye West, Jay-Z (Shawn Carter), and Bunji Garlin (Ian Antonio Alvarez) managed to make a difference and transformed the music industry. I acknowledge other iconic artists such as Michael Jackson, Bob Marley, Aretha

Your Legends As Mentors

Franklin and Madonna (Louise Ciccone) who have all been pioneers in the music industry and created a new landscape of what entertainment looks like today.

From the early days of Jazz; the using of the saxophone and adding the steel pans to the mix, from different cultures. I have explored the evolution of today's music in many different forms and genres. What some young people may call rap or hip-hop or dance hall or soul music, it is nothing new to what I have been exposed to when I was growing up. All these styles of music were laid down from the beginning. Through the legacy of leaders and influences in the music industries.

One iconic leader, Walt Disney, struggled throughout his journey. I have learnt many lessons from Walt Disney's story, and his legacy continues to be an inspiration today; to me, and to many generations of children. As my grandma would say: "you must learn from your lessons!" And it did take me some time to realise that it was not necessarily only my personal lessons or experiences.

In the health and wellness industry, I have had the fortunate to meet members of the Youngevity International Inc. family, allowing me to interact with several of the company's top-earner and distributors. One of the industry's pioneers, Dr. Joel Wallach, and his team, has been on a mission to change the entire wellness industry through education and better options. I was particularly sold on the idea of 'shifting people's thinking' away from the sickness (health) industry into a healthier and wellness thought process.

While these are my experiences, I believe that you too have your own experiences and can identify with people who are making a difference. Perhaps you know others who are on a journey to make a positive change in the world. What about the people in your community? Or even in your workplace environment? That person could be you too. As a 'change agent,' making what may seem minute changes in communities have proven effective to help change entire industries.

Leaders such as Earl Nightingale helped pioneer change in the field of personal development, including tools available to use and their associated publications. In fact, Earl's efforts changed the entire publication industry.

Another influence in people's thought processes and a leader in personal development is Napoleon Hill. When I became familiar with him, my own journey and concepts in education and training transitioned. Many other leaders in the network industries I had the pleasure of meeting reminded me of the work of Napoleon Hill. The 'spill off' extended into network marketing, and public speaking. They too have become influenced by Hill and the legacy of our early leaders.

The music industry has changed in so many ways today. I observe more and more young artists excelling through unconventional methods. They embrace the use of technology, social media, and have improved their social presence in the wider communities.

Some younger and more adventurous have acknowledged the existence of legacy and advanced their social experience. They are doing what many musicians in the past were simply not able to do. However, many young artists have not yet earned their place in society. They are still using earlier formats and blueprints. It is as if the legendary leaders have laid down the structure for industries in the past and are seemingly responsible for what we have today.

We can see the health and wellness industry continuing its progress into something new. Visionary leaders are using technology to help make changes in people's lives. These changes are continuing to take different forms. Although having met many different challenges the wellness arena is keeping up with the mission of what was set out in the past. Veganism, for example, is not exactly new.

Leaders still strive for improving lives all together. You too can *aspire* to create a better healthy lifestyle and help others live much longer through better healthcare ideas, wealth and passing on the legacy of you and your leaders.

WHAT IS YOUR LEGACY?

What is your legacy or purpose? How do you feel about leaving a legacy? Can you identify your purpose in life, your purpose in whatever you are setting out to do? Have you thought about answering the enigmatic questions of: 'Why are you here?' 'Why are you doing this?' Yet these are the type of questions that you may want to ask yourself when you're thinking about your legacy.

On your journey to greatness, perhaps you're wondering: How am I going to get there? What is the best way for me to get there? Or, am I on the right path? Am I doing the right thing? So consider this: 'How do you want to be remembered?' Your resolve will put you in possibly the best comfortable position to fulfil your purpose as you proceed on your journey.

Have you considered at this time, whether you are going to be a trainer, a teacher, or a leader? While some people are managers, others classify themselves as leaders. Leadership is not something you are born with or have a natural talent for; like anything else, leadership can be learned. Whatever you have chosen, and if you are now looking to choose, why not let it be part of your legacy? Consider what you want to be creating for yourself. It may be the way that people are going to remember you. Perhaps it's for something good you've done... let's say the impact you had on other people's lives.

What changes have you made or influenced within your community? Any community. It may be for the ways that you performed or managed a situation. How about the way you led a venture that is unique to you? People will remember you one way or the other. It may be all positive, negative, or a mixture of both. Remember! You are creating this effect. Whatever you create, *you* will leave it behind.

Your legacy could begin now. Your legacy could be something that people are admiring right now. Perhaps it is something you are doing as we speak. Think about the changes you're making, or the impact you're having on people's lives where you work. Perhaps it is your clients, your associates, or even your team members?

Whatever you're doing, be reminded of the impact you leave on people's lives. How are you changing lives? How have you contributed to realising their purpose? Also, think about the aura and the way that others feel when in your presence; this can be an indication of how you will be remembered and what your legacy is going to be like. So, if you're a teacher, be a great teacher that influences other people's lives.

If you're going to show someone your way of doing things, do this to the best of your ability. Share your process with them. If you're going to be a leader, lead with dignity. Lead with integrity and lead by example. Lead with a helping mind. Focus on the outcome and how you are achieving the outcome. This is where you leave your legacy. Your legacy or your story. Those who look back at what you've done and the impact you've created, they are going to remember you for something. Do not hesitate. Act now and create your legacy.

Your Legends As Mentors

Notes

"You become what you think about"
—Earl Nightingale

CHAPTER THREE
WISDOM FROM ELDERS

WHERE TO FIND WISDOM

One great thing about my grandmother was her many experiences, some of which she shared with me. These experiences gave me a different perspective on life and set the scene for some of my lifestyle habits. It also helped in the patterning of my own belief system. My grandma believed in the Holy Bible. And she grew to live according to many biblical and spiritual customs. At least this was what I became familiar with from her experiences.

I heard stories of how my grandma was 'rough' and how she was 'tough' when dealing with some people and their situations. I know she had worked hard. At times, I think to myself about all the legends, 'who hasn't really?' In fact, who do you know that's a legend, that is successful, and who is filled with wisdom that has not had a few indifferences?

Do you know someone that can acknowledge that they have learned from their experiences; someone who could look back and say different versions of stories, yet of whom you could emulate or relate to in different ways?

My grandma didn't only encourage me to read the Bible. In fact, it was because of her way of life, her morals, her ethics, the way she guided me; I believe that she was shaping me and directing me on my path to finding wisdom.

One of my mentors once told me, "Andrew, if you want to find wisdom, why don't you think of the thing that is positive? Every time you think of something that's negative, just don't say it. And if you practise this long enough, you will surely be wise." While it did seem funny to me at the time, laughing at the thought of me doing something even remotely like that, in many ways it turned out to be a wise thing to do.

When I think of my grandma's way of life, I consider her practical sense of living. I relate this at times to the wisdom of Earl Nightingale, whom I acknowledge in my personal development. I like to reflect on his direction and his reminders that we become that which we think about.

Earl Nightingale refers to a number of and particular, quality of books. I find these books are written by individuals with legendary profiles. Earl holds the likes of Dale Carnegie and Napoleon Hill in high regard. I consider these as one of the earlier founders and fathers in personal development and in acquiring wisdom. They will forever remain legendary and are of the elderly that I can refer to when trying to find wisdom.

WHAT IS WISDOM?

One definition I found of wisdom is that it's the quality of having experience and knowledge. Others refer to this as intelligence. This quality of having experience may come in many forms. And wisdom is accessible through other means. It can be words and knowledge based on your own experience. For example, wisdom can be what you've written yourself, your written words.

I often journal write. I aim for daily scribing and would generally explore and reflect on some of my positive experiences. I believe that if someone else is reading this information or able to access my journal, that someone will gain much experience. You will access a wealth of information that gives you a positive view of things.

Another way to think of wisdom and learning is to consider where it comes from. It is embedded in your life experiences. Wisdom comes from the very act of listening without speaking or interrupting. While it is not exactly the only method used in coaching, listening without speaking is very valuable. It's important to note that you shouldn't be listening to people and then making their story part of your own life. If you do that, it can become a burden, so do not let it consume you.

With wisdom, you learn more skills in self-control, in the sense that you gain knowledge to help you develop and manage yourself. You gain self-confidence and grow to the extent of massive development. Ultimately, you will gain insight in line with your personal development.

As I mentioned previously, I keep a daily journal of my own thoughts. Similarly, if you look at other people's work, they are put together in a refined way. It may be used to educate or to advise, and you often find that this knowledge is based on other people. This information is gained from other people and gets compacted in a resourceful way. After looking at it and putting it to use, you can think of it as wise words. This knowledge can be helpful for you as it gets you on a productive path. One that's useful and challenging and helps you to push forward.

Wisdom is something that you will gain over time. But it must come from somewhere and very often it is found within yourself. You can access it when you look through your thought processes. Through meditation, you can look deep within yourself, where you can find a wealth of information and knowledge. This data can be identified and extracted from within your subconscious mind.

Over time, wisdom develops within your thought process. Some people call it intelligence, and you can access it. You convert it and communicate it. You share it with others, and this information can help you and others, by setting them on a more direct and positive path.

CAN WISDOM BE INHERITED

Can we inherit knowledge? Can we inherit brilliance, intelligence or skills? I may not have the best answer for you. So, what do you think? What I know is that if you look within yourself, there are packets of information. Over time, some of this information can become stuck inside you. Some of this information is often accessed daily. When accessed, you can determine whether you have gained any wisdom.

Similarly, these packets of information and the shared drive you possess within you is part of your brilliance. This shared resource that's stuck within you is your intelligence. It is there because you have learned it over time. It's there too because you're learning it right now. It is your actual skills that are growing, and it's there because you stored it.

When you gain knowledge and experience, very often you don't put it all to use. Some of this is called wisdom. In fact, how can you put it all to use at once? In the real sense, when someone asks you a question or when you're looking for the answer to a question, you access files and information that's within your mind, at work. For instance, you access these files and try to put them in a sensible format and in some way regurgitate it back out. This process may help determine your levels of brilliance, intelligence or skillset.

At other times, these files that you contain, these experiences, can be coupled or multiplied to information or knowledge gained from older people, from your legends. When you can merge these packets of information and knowledge, you can create the highest form of wisdom. In this sense, you can see that whether you're a younger or an older person, what you have within you can be validated.

The packets of information, these useful files and resources that you have within you, need to be processed. You need to access data regularly. If it's not enhanced, improved, or upgraded, this information could become obsolete. The information becomes somewhat stale. When the information is outdated, it may still be considered wisdom, even if it is of little use to many people.

Some information that you gain from a very young age or stage in your life stands out as root or foundation knowledge. Perhaps as an infant or a young child growing up, it can become the basis for your skillset. This information, when accessed, is akin to early forms of education and early growth or 'wise sayings,' from other people. In fact, this information, depending on how you access it may be regurgitated.

At less developed stages, information repeated from different forms of material tend to get confused with what people think is yours. As you learn to access these files within you, if you have done very little with them, it may seem as if it's still in the original form. It may be of youthful content yet appearing as if it has grown into an older kind of information. This point is where people may think that you inherited wisdom, as they may identify with some of the sayings that you regurgitated.

HOW TO GAIN WISDOM

I have mentioned earlier that accessing wisdom can be sourced and compiled in different forms. From my grandma, it seemed the Holy Bible was her vast resource. Other times she shared much of her personal experiences and at times, what appeared as my grandma's 'silence' was directional. Some of my other legends refer to what we call history books; other leaders mention their ancestry and influence by their elders.

You can be accessing much from your own past experiences. What is within you: your thought processes, your contemplation and reflections, can reveal an array of thoughts. Yes, I have developed a huge resource in the form of reading. And I believe you can, too.

While reading is not the main form of resource, it is a necessary source. I often refer to a comment made by one of my earlier mentors. He says that, "if you do not read, you have no advantage over a person who cannot read." I too like to add that: "if you are not reading, then what do you actually have to share?"

Now, a lot of people would jump at the opportunity to argue that point. There is the view that you can simply watch videos, or you can listen to others and learn. And I'm happy that you have considered this. While compiling and writing this book, I acknowledge that a considerable stride has been made through audiobooks.

The fact that I am sometimes frequently 'on the move' makes regular reading a bit difficult. By having access to my audiobooks, I'm always learning. Therefore, I consider audiobooks another form of reading. Isn't it amazing that you can be listening, relating, and hearing yourself think? In many ways, reading the actual word does give this similar experience.

You can gain knowledge by learning from others as well. This knowledge can be converted into your source of wisdom. Learning from older people or other legends is another great method. I found that you tend to maintain a current view when engaging and learning from your coaches and mentors within your environment.

I access workshops and training regularly. Through meet-up groups, I can communicate, relate, and share amongst like-minded people. I can stay up-to-date when checking in with other coaches. I am also able to work more fluently with other business partners and people that share similar interests. I tend to learn new things and gain wisdom as a result.

I believe that you often have many packets of improved and enhanced files of information that you store within yourself. I would say that you gain wisdom through your own experiences. On the other hand, learning from others will help you form and develop your own style. Your own experiences. Yes, your own experiences, especially when you track your activities. You can access some of this information and gain from it. You can become even more knowledgeable, wise, and develop further over time.

Which wise elderly person should you choose?

I continuously talk about *Aspiring, As My Grandma Would Say*. It's important that I mention that I have been engaged with other legends, in addition, and apart from my grandma. I have had the privilege and have taken the opportunity to converse with a more comprehensive, older, and more experienced community of individuals. I say more experienced and not just older as some people have grown in age. And while they're considered elderly, their experiences are not exactly positive.

While you can learn from anyone or anyone's experience, what you learn is very important. Choose wisely. I'll like you to consider your chosen path. Let's examine or think of your own 'mind files'. Do you have the thought process of being successful? Do you want to be able to access successful knowledge and learning? Do you want to be able to gain knowledge? Then why not learn from others who have walked down that path? Others who have and can show that they were successful.

It's important to note that success here does not necessarily mean monetary success, only. You can certainly learn from older people who are considered rich. Their experience is a definite form of projecting a successful outcome. However, while the rich and wealthy have similar experiences, it is essential to recognise that wealthy individuals are not only rich in terms of money.

This is where I refer to the older people who have had massive impacts on their communities and have been greatly finantially successful; mostly due to their leadership and the other effective changes within communities at the time. Wisdom manifests itself in different ways. Gaining wisdom or accessing experiences of wise older people is necessary. This interaction is more beneficial for a more focused mind while you're seeking your own aspirations. And for this reason you must stand out from the rest with your uniqueness.

It is in the wise elderly that we gain specific measures of wisdom. This is sometimes seen as 'fool proof'. These experiences are filled with varying amounts of positivity, elevating into a richness of wisdom. The wisdom within your own personal development, in your own progress and in your growth. Why not seek out some elderly people in your circle of influences?

THE WISE GRANDMA

I've mentioned earlier that learning from my grandma and Aspiring, As My Grandma Would Say was not only a matter of growing up. Neither was it solely about learning or doing and acting on what was said to me. The 'wise grandma,' is potentially, and particularly in many cases; your elderly, and in your choice, the people you admire. They are of senior ages. Within them, there are certain qualities that you may want to acknowledge and that you can identify with. Some qualities will be unique to you and that individual and within your connections.

My grandma showed me the qualities of humbleness. Humbleness concerning the sense of peace, calm, and 'progressive stillness.' During this period, my grandma was generally accessible, yet she was still very protective. I often reminisce about the calm atmosphere during her periods and stages of humbleness. My reflection signals a sense of her spirituality. And sometimes I think of my grandma's level of integrity as a true sense of her identity.

The identity of 'the wise grandma', is someone who walked the walk and talked the talk. She is not afraid of anyone looking into her life. The wise grandma will hold a high level of respect because she is true to herself and true to others. The wise grandma will live a real attractive life. There will be that sense of transparency in what she did or is doing.

An integral part of 'the wise grandma' is that she learned from her life experiences and from overcoming her failures. In fact, her openness will establish that she is trustworthy. And as my grandma would say: 'choose wisely.' Select the older person that you choose to admire in your life, even if you do not admire or respect all their specific qualities.

Right now, yes, right this moment, you may want to rethink, revisit, or rekindle with that older person. That someone with a certain sense of attitude. How about that someone you can think of that is distinctive to you. Yes, that wise elderly.

Growing up with my grandma appears to sometimes allow for my learning to have a sense of adaptability. Perhaps more like significant levels of attitude adjustment strategies. Sometimes this attitude change seems to come as a result of my grandma's humbleness, her trustworthy, and her attitude altogether. Grandma's spirituality would say a lot too.

I do not refer to a specific religion or church denomination, or your personal belief in God, or your higher power. I do, however, take this time to reflect and instil in you that there must be something that you believe in: A higher form, your sense of creation, or some sense of moral stance. Trust that instinct if you need to. I do believe that 'the wise grandma' would identify and have a sense of spirituality, even if it is not religious.

If you are finding it difficult to connect, why not admire your own grandma or another older person. During their periods of rest observe them. Have a look at the expressions on their face. Where does it take them? What is it doing for them? What are they thinking about? What have their experiences been like? Why not ask them? The wise grandma is who you choose to connect with.

GRANDMA'S WISE SAYINGS

I love thinking about my grandma's sayings. At first, I would hear the phrases and laugh about it and sometimes repeat it or hear someone else saying it and laugh at it. It started with simple things like "who don't hear, would feel (the consequences)." In the early stages, I even heard phrases like: 'if you live in a glasshouse, don't throw stones" I later heard this sung by Bob Marley & the Wailers.

I often remember things with a smile. At other times I have awakened with thoughts of my grandma's sayings in my head, and these have grown with me, well into my current day experiences. When I hear other 'life' coaches, other thought leaders and change-makers, refer to, say, biblical terms or wise sayings, I would have thought of my grandma's saying. This connection makes me think even deeper.

One of the things that I often smile about is that saying of 'what goes around, comes around.' If you're into music, one of the later forms of this 'saying' I've heard is from the late Robert Nester or Bob Marley. He would say: 'what goes around, comes forward around.'

Other recording artistes like "Sizzla Kalonji (Miguel Collins)" and "Chronixx (Jamar McNaughton)" alluded to this too, especially when in deep musical expressions. This term is often mentioned by other 'deep thought' and inspirational reggae artists in music arenas. I find it has a spiritual connection, when expressed. The phrase is a biblical saying and is used by many who are not referring to the Bible.

Another saying that my grandma often referred to was: 'you reap what you sow.' In one of my latest book readings and personal development journey activities, I repeatedly heard Earl Nightingale refer to this phrase. While growing up, it's been a phrase that my mother often used. Other older people have used this to remind me of my own experience. My own doing and my own actions, and as it relates to my expected outcomes.

Again, my grandmother would say things like, "You make your bed; you sleep in it." And while that sometimes made me smile,

I would often think it was a made-up story. Later, as I visit and chat with other older people and hear other people refer to phrases or sayings like this, I think my grandma's sayings were no joke. As you think of your own sayings and your own experiences, why not consider your own sayings and influences growing up. Being exposed to your own elderly influences and experiences, coupled with your own reading can give you your own legendary access, as wise sayings.

One of the interesting things I've heard my grandma says to me is, "Seek and you shall find." Repeatedly and of late, I have been listening and looking at one of the proliferate leaders in personal development. He has been referred to as an 'all-time best' motivational speaker, the well-known Leslie Brown. He has been continuously reminding me to apply to this fact that: 'you seek, and you shall find.'

While I have shared some of my own grandma's sayings, they are also some of the sayings of other legends. These include other older people who I believe have had life-changing experiences. Some of these influencers have had a huge impact on business leaders, parents and children. I hope that these wise sayings will have an impact on you, and your life-changing decisions, as you become more aware of others wise sayings.

MY WISE LEARNING CURVE

My learning curve came from some hilarious experiences growing up. At one point in my life, I was struggling with reading. This struggle got to the extent, that as soon as I opened a book, even before starting to read, I would feel sleepy. Parts of my experience seemed to adopt a psychological type of effect where I wanted to close my eyes in a matter of seconds. I'd eventually close the book as I'd get sleepy and tired. I believe at some point avoidance of opening books became the better option.

While a considerable part of this book reading effect probably developed the fact that I hated reading, it became evident in my thought process that, it was, in fact, a physical thing. I was struggling with weakened vision as I later found out. It took me a long time to realise that I needed to wear glasses too. I needed to correct my eyesight. I needed to look after my eyes and myself. At the time, I lacked the financial means and allowed pride and delay to take the lead in what seemed like unnecessary suffering.

I then chose to learn through my experiences by working with other people. I volunteered my time and services and was able to recognise changes in my learning curve. Some of these changes came from the fact that I was learning about different people's experiences. I was now exposed to their different cultures, their belief systems and their way of life. I was learning from other people's stories and building my own confidence.

Volunteering my time to help others allowed me to meet and connect with other people. I started to develop my own networks. My own goals and Life vision started to take form too. In some ways, my own sense of wisdom had begun to develop in a unique and exciting way. Over some time, I had an interesting period of growth as I made certain choices.

During my time working within the care industry, I developed a different sense of purpose. This purpose became evident when I started volunteering in New York, the USA. I would travel to various places, learning the 'subways' train networks, meeting many different people, and being in a variety of situations throughout the busyness.

Aspire As My Grandma Would Say

I would often compare different periods of my time living in the Caribbean, learning the 'wise sayings', and not paying much attention to what was being said at the time. Yes! That time when I was connecting with the elderly. I later recognised what I was meant to be preparing for. A huge change in my learning curve was developing over the significant travels to different cultures, in different environments, behaviours, and countries.

I have compared the vision of the older people I've met and interacted within Canada to other territories. I have noticed similarities, particularly the calmness on Sunday mornings. And just after the midday period, I noticed a period of joy being emitted as interactions among small groups of older people seemed to pop up, especially in food areas. This may include a mealtime or over a cup of tea, coffee, or snack.

As I recall, some of the older people I have visited at their care homes or in hospices, I mainly think of the times sitting and listening to some of them. This time was another learning period for me. Once, I conversed with a group from within the West Palm Beach areas in Florida, USA. I remember how appreciative some of the older people felt and how they expressed their gratitude. It meant a great deal to them to have someone to interact with and listen to their stories.

You may not see the value in a few minutes of your time. But your few minutes may mean the world to others who are willing to teach you something valuable. I reflect on the huge experience gained while working within the care industry in the UK. I have met several older people, visiting them in their homes, even some frail seniors who would feel honoured to share their stories with me.

Several older people would express that sharing their experiences with me often cheered them up, as the memories will uplift their moods. At times it made me smile as I get that sense of joy in making them smile with their stories and getting them out of their low mood periods.

At times, I would look at an elderly individual experiencing pain and wonder how they were still laughing. I have developed a huge admiration and respect as they always appreciate life. Some of them are so joyful to be around. And this has opened my airwaves and vibe of wanting to learn more about their appreciation for life. While I learn on this curve of life experiences, wisdom has followed. Now it's your turn.

Why not reflect on your own experiences. On your own learning curve. Use the note areas to write as you brainstorm. Write your thoughts and personal reflections.

Aspire As My Grandma Would Say

Notes

"It's not enough to be in the right place at the right time, you must be the right person in the right place at the right time'

—T Harv Eker

CHAPTER FOUR
SUCCESSFUL PATHWAYS

PATHWAYS TO SUCCESS

I like to think of my grandma as a charismatic person. She was generally friendly, and a woman filled with peacefulness and calm. I remember on occasions when she would receive visits by adults in the community. Sometimes older people expressed that they received a warm, welcoming feeling, and a sense of comfort from my grandma. She had a way about her that made you smile, even now as I think about her. My grandma would make you discover some happy feeling, most of the time.

I've seen my grandma's sense of charisma with many successful leaders. As I compare her to some, we call out as leaders or refer to as diplomats and influential people; I recognise that my grandma possessed one of the essential keys to the pathway of success. My grandma had a special kind of charisma about her, and she didn't go out trying to look great, or be great, in the public eyes.

My grandma showed her interest in you. Naturally, something attracted other people to her. She connected with others in a sociable manner, and in a simple way too. Grandma's education wasn't top-notch. Well, she didn't possess qualifications in the form of degrees and masters or PhDs. She didn't have a huge amount of qualifications. However, she was trained and experienced in what she knew and did.

My grandma was a nurse in her profession. She looked after many people with care, and from what I learned, she made them feel valuable. My grandma was interested. Perhaps her charisma was a driving force in which she helped to look after people, especially mothers. Although my grandma performed a midwifery role, she dedicated extra interest and cared for you.

I am fascinated at some mother's sharing their stories, following the birth of their children. They are even sharing stories when their child has grown into adulthood. The experiences are memorable, even though the child may have gone off on their own pathways. I listen to mothers talk about my grandma and how she served them.

When I think of the many qualities of leaders, I sense what is necessary, especially, from my grandma's experiences. Perhaps it was her giving, and perhaps it was her way of just actioning and getting on with things and making things happen. My grandma gave value to people. She served.

One thing I knew about my grandma is that she didn't like the senseless, and meaningless 'small talks.' She tended to get straight to the point. Grandma wanted to know what it was you wanted. She'd rather be in silent, quiet time, than just being idle. And even though she was someone who acted, she liked taking her time out for silence. Perhaps for meditation?

If grandma had something to do on a specific day, grandma would just set off and get it done. She would engage in her silence and her quiet time and plan, more so, during her meditation period. Very often, I've been taught similar qualities of my grandma by my coaches and mentors, Some of which I can share with you.

When you can plan,, it's almost as if you're already on that journey. When you set off on the actual journey, you already know what you're on about. You already know what steps you must take, where you're meant to go, and where you should be going. You need to act. One important point to note, though, is that when you plan it is not always about the plan. It is more about the person you will become when you follow the process. It is about the lessons on your pathways to your success.

MY SUCCESS JOURNEYS

I've really had some 'chilled-out' experiences on my life journeys. I like to smile and chuckle too, at times. Thinking back, I can see variations in some of my mother and my grandmother's behaviours and habits. I also realise that many of my mother's ways, and her behaviours are not necessarily inherited or learnt from my grandmother, her mum.

I have come to accept that my experiences are parts of my story. Similarly, your experiences will be parts of your personal story. Most of our experiences are unique in such a way that it tells a particularly different story. Your selected pathways are sacred and are significant parts of your success journey. If you think of sharing someone else's story, then why not share your story too.

When I share my story or my journey with others, it may have some of your experiences or influences within and vice versa. Either way, it will still be my experiences and my journey or story. I like the idea of learning from other people's experiences. My success journey will always have that uniqueness about it, no matter what. As I indicated, growing up with my grandmother was unique to me. And today, I can use a lot of what she said, a lot of what she's done, most of what she's taught me. No matter what their story has been, I can use this to create my own success journey. What about you?

As I think of some of the books I've read, I often connect with this with some of the people I've met. I sometimes imagine how they will impact my journey as I go forward. I can think of how the people I've met have impacted my life and how they've helped direct me on my path. I will always appreciate how their direction has brought me to where I am today. I have taken that journey, and I am taking the necessary steps. I have carried on with that path, and I am choosing my paths toward other successful journeys.

In the same way, learning from other leaders does have its merits. The way that they've done, it is particularly unique to me too. It has also had huge influences on the path that I have taken. This included how my journey was taken and some of the trips I have taken across to other countries. Other people's journeys and their stories; have all helped me to create my own success journey.

It was in meeting some of the very people I work with today that brought me on paths of my successes. Their guidance has helped me to choose. Their influences assisted me in getting to my 'endpoints,' where I thought I could just chill-out. Sometimes endpoints are often where you may think you would want to get to at some time in your life's journey. Where you may want to 'chill-out.' Yes! This point is often the time where you can relax and refresh; however you must revamp. You must revive and go again.

It could be on a daily, a monthly or quarterly period. You will want to experience some chill time, some rest time. As people like to take holidays, perhaps every year, this could turn into a remarkable success shoal or target. It can take a form where you travel out of your neighbourhood. Similarly, it could be a remote area in the countryside or even where you're living, right now. Just taking time out to experience something new is part of your journey. This time too, will remain part of your success journey.

WHICH PATH TO TAKE

I remember one time in discussion, my grandmother telling me: "Andrew, you'll have to choose. Your time will come. One day, someday you will have to choose." This saying always comes as a reminder to me. As some of the belief systems my grandma had, I didn't exactly believe. I always had the way that I wanted to follow. I didn't quite understand the angle my grandma was referring to at the time.

I would often challenge and question my grandma's phrases. I would ask a series of questions like; "Why is this so? Why is that this way? Why is it not this or that way?" And rather than giving me a straight answer, she would turn to me and say: "Don't worry, your time will come."

And so, as time passed, I chose. I had to take my path, and I had to choose a way that I believed was going to take me on my journey to success. I learned to stop comparing myself with other people. I learned to set my own bars and set my own targets. I set my own levels of achievements, especially mentally. I have chosen my own paths according to the very legends that you and I may have known of, today. Robert Kiyosaki has been a huge influence in my life. His publications have impacted me, and in the financial education I have acquired.

T. Harv Eker has played an instrumental part in my mindset about money and changing my investing practices. T. Harv's principles have helped me create new habits. I have learnt to adjust my mindset whenever I have been thinking about money and spending.

Aspire As My Grandma Would Say

When I met the award-winning author and international speaker, Vishal Mojaria, he inspired me to get my book published. His humbleness, meeting him in person and the way he stood out, intrigued me. His posture reminded me of the person I was aspiring to be, one who was confident, charismatic and firm. It was the stature of the person I wanted to become, several years before.

Mainly, I will tell you that you too must emulate and imitate. I am saying that you also must choose. And as my grandma taught me, encouraged, and directed me, I too believe that you must choose a path. When reminded or faced with that vision of what it is you want, Stop! Take a breath, examine and focus in that direction. Take that decision you make and turn it into action.

I remember the early days when having casual conversations with my grandma. I would listen to her talk about my uncles, their journeys and their sailing experiences on ships. She enjoyed going on about their experiences at sea. While I found it admirable and of eager interest, she reminded me of an important fact. She would say: "boy, you don't have to choose their path. Choose your own path to have your own successes."

As I have highlighted, you will need to make your choice based on what you want and what you feel is right for you. And today, as I think back on my grandma's ways and how she inspired me to take my own path, I am encouraging you. Choose to get on your own levels. I am insisting that you too must consider which path you want to take, and which way is right for you.

WHEN TO PART WAYS

At some point in your life journey, you must go your separate paths, your different ways. You will need to gain some level of independence. You must take your own path and create your 'story.' You might do this as an adult, or even as a young person. After a bit of learning, or even some 'trial and error.'

After having a few hiccups and a few challenges, you may want to or get to a point when you need to choose. You may even decide to part ways right now, today. As my grandma inspired me, I acted and chose specific paths. In choosing different paths, you may be carrying 'unwanted baggage' in your life. Stuff that needs dealing with, especially from other people.

Sometimes we want to go our separate ways, and it seems difficult. You want to go on your own paths and obstacles appear. You may have a friend, partner, or it might be your significant other. It could even be a husband or wife stopping you. Sometimes it is a special relationship or friendship that will seem too important. Either way, at some point you need to take a huge step, a huge change, or that huge decision, and 'do you. 'And I do know that at times it may be difficult.

You may be in a marriage, and I'm not soliciting you to choose to leave, hurt or 'ill-treat 'your partner. You may be in a business relationship or another type of long-term friendship, and you want to choose to go your own way, your own path. You may be thinking of choosing to do this at the most opportune time, at a time that it's necessary.

Even when that necessary time may not seem to be right now, right this minute, it may just be the best time. When do you part ways in your relationship? What about with your business partner? When would you say is the best time to say: "Hey, this is not for me.", Are you afraid to accept it?

Where do you ask or decide: hey, is now that time? It may be today, tomorrow. You may either be procrastinating, getting overwhelmed, or getting confused. If you are lingering and being hesitant, remember, time is passing you by.

When you part ways is when you make that decision. When you decide to aspire to greater heights, you will exceed to another level and on another journey. When you part ways is where you choose your successful pathway.

Why not decide right now, at this moment? Why not take the decision today! Why not part ways with what's holding you back. Reach out! Find out how you can get help with this if you are struggling. Release yourself from what is stopping you. Choose your successful pathway today.

SUCCESS THINKING

Your decision to think successful is one of the most significant choices you'll ever take in your life. That decision you made will change or create a new thought process altogether. One decision helped me to connect with a community called the Miracle Morning. This community connection came as a result of my reading (physical) books and listening to audiobooks, as I followed the directions of my mentors. This process has furthered my thinking at different levels, and I continue to expand in my personal development and growth processes.

You will encounter periods in your life where you need to think outside of your spectrum. You will need to think outside of your immediate environment. Some people say that you should think big and I would indicate that you need to think bigger.

At times, I focused on what a vision of my thoughts looked like, and it resembled my grandma sat in her veranda overlooking the ocean. Although she was in her retirement age and stages in her life, her thinking was a massive part of her daily routine. I have emulated this idea too.

At times, my grandma appeared as if she stared at nothing. Sometimes it appeared as if she's just staring at the beauty of the ocean, or at the garden below, or across the mountains. At odd times she would make simple remarks, particularly of something that seemed random. Grandma would make mention of a ship that was passing by, and it may be miles out of my sight.

Grandma liked to speak of some of the birds that flew across the sky. She had this way of just being in silent thoughts. Almost like a meditative type mode. Sometimes her silence would seem to bring a smile on her face, and occasionally, she would indicate that 'I know you are there.' This thought tends to remind me of the idea that 'thinking must be hard work' of which I chuckle at the phrase when I encounter visions of the smile on grandma's face.

My grandma seemed at times to live 'within herself.' Although she was deeply contemplative and spiritual, thoughts of her dispositions remind me of some things I encountered most recently. I started a new idea of looking more into my thoughts, and controlling the flow of my thoughts more directly, and separating myself from my own emotions.

I was learning to focus more on my thought process and how to take charge of my feelings. To be more in control of what I'm thinking about. This control came as a result of my decisions to think more consciously of the journey of my success path.

THE RIGHT ATTITUDE FOR SUCCESS

The right attitude for success has been referred to often in different ways. While this can be said in a variety of ways, the right attitude for success is an extension of your thinking process. Your thought process needs to encourage you to take yourself away from some of your own thinking. What you hear inside of your head may often be your self-talk. It is important to be aware of what you are listening to, whether it is internal or external.

To take charge of your self-talk and to be in control of what you're thinking about, requires having the right attitude. Success is where you choose to act. Always think about that journey. However, the processes must be action focused. A thought process of this type consists of maintaining a 'no excuse' type of attitude. The right attitude for success involves you being mindful of your time. It is necessary that you have a system of how you will create your daily tasks.

You need to develop some action routines for your journeys. I continue to start my 'full-on daily journeys with some periods of silence. I do this mainly in the early mornings. I like to start my day in this manner, with a bit of hydration, meditation, and visualisation. These are only some of the actions I take before I get fully connected to my technological devices.

Before I get connected to the rest of the world, I prepare myself first. I have a period of silence, create my own atmosphere, and get into my 'flow.' I tend to get my attitude recharged and adjusted and filled with energy. I will create a smile before I set off on my day's journey. I often visualise what and how some of the tasks will be. I prepare for successful focus into the day, and to continue that path to success, as part of my routine.

As my day is beginning, I like to feel recharged and filled with energy. Preferably not with coffee or any type of caffeine products. Instead, I connect with my own sense of being. I create readiness in my mind. I connect within my senses. I refer to this as my 'flow.' A natural feeling of wanting to start my day and with success in mind.

I tend to focus on some actions I will take, and I tend to look at the processes within my 'mind's eye.' I picture the steps and actions I will take throughout the day. This system gives me a feeling of enthusiasm and of wanting to pursue the tasks or activity. I then transition my flow into the process of the rest of my day.

Why not reflect on the way you start your day? Do you start with a positive attitude? Do you have routine activities?

YOUR MAIN RESOURCES

So now, why not consider some of the things you will need to think of when taking a journey. In fact, to start your successful pathway process. I believe you can agree that you're not going to have a successful pathway without first having to plan and take that journey; right? So, what do you take on this journey?

Your main resources are what you have. Yes! I said it! Your main resources are the very things you have access to and what you can access. Your main resources include what you've learned. It is made up of people you've met, the books you've read. The things you've learned and can implement. Your main resources include the people you can access. The things that you can access are extras or add-ons.'

I believe that your main resources are mostly within you and in your immediate reach. Your limbs, your senses, and thinking. What do you really need to carry around with you today? What do you have to access to create a successful pathway? Think of the 'What!'

Who do you aspire to be, today? Perhaps you need a checklist, check. Perhaps you have one, two, three; three items of those five or six things listed on your checklist, yes; check. And maybe the next two or three things you need to do is to speak to someone and get a drink.

At first, someone may have the answer for you. This person may have referred you to a book, or some additional resources you needed right now. And now, the next person recreates that next check on your checklist. Remember this; you already have what you need.

What if you thought that you know all you need right now? And that you've covered your checklist. Then you realise that this checklist is only part of the resources that you started with. Who created your checklist? Who created these resources? If you take a few seconds to just think and realise that, within yourself, to create a checklist physically, you didn't have to move; you didn't have to choose another path. You can do this through your own thoughts.

What you may come to acknowledge at times is that your main resources are almost a mental thing. Your main resources can be accessed through your own thoughts. Through your own thinking, is it not always evident that the resources you brought to light were what you previously made a note of? It means you were able to access your items through your thinking, initially.

Your own success pathway is embedded in the main resources that are frequently stuck within your headspace. This pathway may come out in different forms. It may be awakened perhaps on paper, or on a device, and you can put it all together in a small package. It is imperative that you take the first step, and that you take the first action. Your main resources can be written out or expressed, from within you.

WHAT IF I CHOOSE ANOTHER PATH?

As I sat contemplating, reminiscing of conversations I've had with my grandma, I took a few minutes to consider the what-ifs, the buts, the maybes. I dismiss them all. I think to myself, "What if I choose another path?" What about you? So, what if you choose another path?

Imagine for a moment, that this is the path you're on, your successful pathway. Consider too, that this is the path that you aspire to be on. Your path to create your own success journey.

So, this is the path you're taking right now. Imagine if you deviate, if you choose otherwise, so what? Like I asked you, think! What-if? What if you spend enough time, perhaps now, tomorrow, or the beginning of your day? Can you visualise this new outcome? Think about your journey. What do you want to do? What actions do you want to take? What action can you do right now?

It's during this visualising process or period that you're going to realise that you can choose any path that you want to take. If you take a few moments now, why not let me take you on through a period of meditation. A period of silence. A period of intentional relaxation to recharge and let your mind focus. Let's focus on the journey that got you here. Yes, at this present time and place. Do check that it is safe for you to do this now, please, before you close your eyes.

And now, think of where you're planning to be, where you want to be. That place where you're going to be at, Yes, take a moment to stop everything else, and focus. Focus on your journey, your new path. Can you smell anything different? Can you feel and taste something strange or familiar? What can you see? Who is there with you?

As you are still here, do consider that it's in this period of thinking and deciding that you're able to choose another path. It is not advisable now that you start worrying or getting confused, over anything. Avoid creating extra stuff or creating more obstacles on your journey. Let's revisit something within your lifestyle. Let's touch on that what-if period of activities.

What-ifs could be doubts that you created within your mind. Your what-ifs could be your blockages. If you have contemplated or want to choose another path, then let's do it. Choose and act immediately. Act today.

If you decide to absent your mind from these what-ifs, you can still choose another path. There are no what-ifs when you decide to act and set off on your journey. You must commit, though. You must be focused, and you must have some levels of faith. You must follow a certain process. You will need to let go and do it. Act and laugh as you go forward, confidently on your path.

Notes

"Kim and I do not live below our means. We believe living below our means only depress our spirits"

—Robert T kiyosaki

CHAPTER FIVE

WEALTH CREATION HABITS

WEALTHY THINKING

Wealthy thinking is so common amongst the rich, the wealthy, and the successful. Several other things are in common with wealthy thinking. I know now that they think in terms of results. For them, results show that they have a certain mindset. It's almost, like a mind IQ.

Some say they set a bar, like a threshold. Many times, they seem to have a way of doing things that's quite simple. Similarly, I tend not to focus on all the little things and instead, keep the big picture. Their mindset seems set on a focal point, as the main target.

Wealthy thinking is not only for people who have money, who are rich, or who are wealthy. Wealthy thinking is something that any successful person should do regularly. If you want to create wealthy habits, then you should have wealthy mentality. As I indicated earlier, why not look within yourself. Search and control your thoughts, and do not allow your mind to take charge. Take the lead in what you do, in what you think and how you feel. These are all elements of wealthy thinking.

Aspire As My Grandma Would Say

Wealthy thinking is about lifting yourself higher. I know this through several experiences too. Do you have your own idea of wealthy thinking or what it should be? I've been working on these with several people who are considered wealthy in terms of their financial self-worth. In fact, in terms of their monetary value and relation to their results. When I attend workshops, I attend workshops led by individuals who are successful in what they do.

My mentors have achieved success at different levels, and they think in terms of wealth. They think residual income and they think passive income. My mentors think of not having a daily routine in the sense of a job. However, they do have a pattern in which they follow that is quite systematised.

Their daily system often starts with a very energising routine. Similarly, the day starts with planning, visualizing, and affirmations. Exercise is a daily part of their thinking, and as such, they have certain habits in which they follow and which they live by. I have now adopted many of these in my thought processes too.

Wealthy thinking is about you having a clear conscience. It involves you having controlled ways of doing your tasks. Of you performing your role, and of carrying out your day to day activities, consciously, and fully aware. Thinking in terms of your wealth is also thinking in terms of your health. There's no wealthy thinking without healthy thinking. As such, at the start of your day, think healthily.

At the start of wealthy people's day, they have a refreshing and invigorating intake of foods. New trends in food seem to influence the start of the day. This healthy food intake helps them to feel energised. It helps to maintain some of their activities throughout the day. It helps them to carry on. As if their life depends on what they take into their bodies and what they are looking to achieve.

WHY HAVE HABITS?

So, if you want to have wealth, would it be right to say, you must have some wealth habits? You need to have the habit of practising, 'repeated action.' The habit of doing and carrying on your day to day activities. Systematically, you need to maintain, develop, and carry on your day to day activities, with some sense of routine. This action is necessary since habits are created after you start and continue to progress in a repeated manner.

As you create motion, and as you start thinking and living at different levels, this will put you on track, Towards your success, and what you do on a day to day basis. You tend to develop into a routine and set patterns, causing a habit to form. Why not consider this reasoning: 'Being habitual means you will tend to lessen your time to wonder, to think, and to avoid mingling with unnecessary tasks.'

We all have habits. Sometimes we can refer to these habits as our day to day practice. At times we don't even think about some actions as 'our habits.' We may look at our patterns as normal. Think about it for a moment. Our getting up, getting ready, getting on the move and arriving at our destination. With very little thought, we tend to carry out these motions of activities regularly, not recognising that it's habitual.

This continued motion comes from practising and making routine advances. This action comes from a regular pattern of behaviour of habits. Can you identify some of your regular 'dismissed' type of behaviours, your habits?

We should all have habits to develop and to become better at what we do. As my grandma would remind me as a young man: 'wealthy people don't behave like we do.' Wealthy people tend to create intentional habits of thoughts. They carry out their day to day activities in such a way that they don't have to spend time. As my grandma would (often) say: 'boy, stop wasting your time.'

My grandma would go on to say; "by the way, 'where' you get all this time from?" I was learning from an early stage that you tend to: waste time, trying to think about the unnecessary and less-productive matters. Having habits tends to eliminate a lot of time-consuming and time-wasting activities. With habits, there is less deviation and more focus on a path. You concentrate on your tasks, and your goals.

A habit is necessary for the continuation and smooth process of your activities and your routine tasks. Having a system of a positive mindset is beneficial to your mind's health too. Your body and mind need to maintain constant motion, constant activities, and consistent practices. Naturally, you will create habits. You will have habits because you follow a set chain of actions. Your chain of thoughts, in turn, creates focus. And, developing habits allows for an effortless flow of getting things done.

WHAT IS WEALTH?

I am sure that there is no one true definition of wealth. One overall view is that wealth is seen as a comfortable state of living, where there is less worry of day to day expenses and better day to day well-being. And yes, wealth reduces some concerns as it relates to your lifestyle. I mentioned the idea less worry. With wealth, although nothing stays unchanged, there is a pattern of income, and a process of receiving. There is also an intentional act that involves conscious and intentional giving.

Wealth includes a continuous flow of actions. There are constant transactional activities taking place when you're in a state of wealth. When your health continues to grow is when your wealth continues to extend, not the other way around. Your state of mind tends to elevate in relation to your income. As you look after your health, you can experience a truly blessed, state of mind. This statement is true whether you are religious, spiritual, atheist or deity.

Wealth is a result of an activity. You can feel it or experience it physically in the rewarded sense. Most commonly it is a state of receiving, especially when monetarily rewards are valued as exchange. These can be called assets. Assets are things you tend to own that have a tangible value assigned to them. Yes, your car, your mobile devices, your food, even your body parts. Oh-please smile, with that last thought.

Residual income is often referred to as a 'constant inflow.' Some 'fun-loving' wealthy marketers would say: it comes in a consistent pattern that you will enjoy. It may be useful for me to mention that residual income is income where you don't often have to carry out a specific daily task to receive inflows. Residual income is something that you do once, and then you receive income for that one thing, continuously. This type of income is the path to true wealth.

One simple form of residual income that I love and enjoy comes from being an author. As it regards wealth, being an author, whether it be writing a book, segment or articles or making music, or being a performer, you can create your own wealth. It is where you tend to create an art piece in one instance, and you're able to reuse this one outcome, this one activity, to constantly receive income, receive a reward.

There is one catch to how you choose to create residual wealth. You must share something of value. That's it! As my grandma would say: 'you must make a positive impact on others' lives.

Wealth, for some successful individuals, is being able to provide financially towards supporting their choices of charitable activities. Achieving lifestyles with wealth may mean that some form of philanthropy tends to follow. This is common when a level of satisfying achievement is realised.

While you don't have to be rich or only at a wealthy state to provide or support a well-needed cause, being wealthy can release you. Wealth can provide a huge release from the unnecessary worry of being able to contribute toward 'your causes' and give charitable support. Very often with wealth, there are levels of lifestyles that you tend to live that remind you of what you've done. Particularly, what you've gained at such a level of achieving, sometimes, you can think that with your expertise, it's a 'surreal feeling,' while making a difference in people's lives.

WHERE TO CREATE WEALTH

Creating wealth must be a personal choice. It must be personal to you. Creating wealth must be personal to your achievement, your desires, and your way of life. Being wealthy must be a decision that you make for yourself. It must have a huge impact on your mindset as within yourself. You will need to make a conscious decision for wealth. Frequently I would say proclaim that which you want to create.

If you want to create wealth, you should be able to declare it. As a great mentor, and one of my personal and business coaches who continues to direct me, would say, make a declaration that you will create wealth 'no matter what'. You can create wealth within your mind, within your thought processes and yourself. Creating wealth is personal, so it needs to be a decision that you make for you, personally.

Wealth Creation Habits

One of the things I admired about my grandma is that she didn't 'boast' about her wealth. Neither did she proclaim it publicly. As my grandma would say: 'Live a wealthy life, with what you already have.'

I indicated earlier that wealth might not simply be a matter of lifestyle to you. It may be a natural elevation of yourself. You can create wealth in your profession, and especially if you're self-employed. If you're a business owner, you create wealth from your expertise and in solving a problem. Whether you're an accountant, a physician, a technician, a mechanic, someone into research or the legal services, you can create wealth with whatever work you do.

Whatever you do to serve people, do it with good intentions. When you do this, it creates a feeling of wealth for that next person and within you. Since creating wealth is a personal choice, I believe it is a conscious aspect of your well-being. It is a part of your life that you will make real if you choose to. Do remember, creating wealth is not by default.

Many people still believe that you can only create wealth through business ventures. Sometimes, it may become too difficult for you to create wealth within yourself or by yourself. I will suggest that there's always a possibility of a joint venture or JV as we refer to it, if it is for yourself, especially monetarily. Or within yourself, you don't have to do it alone. I often share with my coaching clients: Reach out! Reach up!

Creating wealth could be in your home country. It could be from overseas or international investments. It can be from trying to assist someone else with their venture as a silent partner and as a 'silent' or active investor. It can be a family member. It can be in the form of someone just backing a project or a business activity. Whatever it is you are choosing, avoid restricting yourself.

Aspire As My Grandma Would Say

Limiting beliefs and negative self-talk will do this and create blockages for you. Your choice of creating wealth will not solely happen for you in a financial institution. Trying to save your money is not often the best practice for many reasons. Some of these you may be fully aware of.

Think of the returns on your investment too. It's sometimes deemed as selfish if you were to try to save your money. You can laugh at this too. You'll rarely find a bank or a financial institution giving you an adequate return on your investment or a huge interest rate. The returns and rewards on your savings will vary too. Depending on whether this exists in very few countries, very few territories, it is not very popular, and it's not very attractive in most cases.

My grandma proved this well in her lifestyle. Owning property or real estate seems to have its merits and provide for possibilities. Why not start creating wealth for you for yourself? Start within your mindset, within your thought process. And if you're not a professional in a field, why not look at the possibility of starting something with someone else? A JV or joint venture and, respectively, a business venture.

WHERE TO FIND WEALTH

In its simplest form, wealth is most of the time all around you. The richness of your communities, and your environments, have wealth written or spelt all over it. Wealth can be found safely within ourselves. To find this wealth within yourselves, you will need to access it. To find wealth within yourself, you need to find the right attitude and the right mindset.

You will need to use your thinking, to control your thoughts and control what your mind is saying to you. What you are thinking and what you are visualising can be aligned. What you are telling yourself in the sense of affirmations and your self-talk, needs to be in your everyday language. The words you use need to be positive and uplifting.

Wealth is often found in investments. It's one of the more popular areas of wealth too. I will also refer here to investment in the sense of observing how everyone else sometimes seems to be splurging their money and their interests everywhere, where others tend to direct their know-how in other people's affairs. I smile at times when I refer to other people's affairs. Note here that wealth is something you don't usually hold for yourself. It is shared, and it is grown. Wealth is developed massively by pools of other people's money.

I mentioned earlier that you could find wealth in many JVs or joint ventures, such as a 'collaborations.' Frequently I refer to master-minding. This collaboration is most effective when you can bring a group of people together with different knowledge, different expertise, and with one, similar focus, on a particular outcome. This is an exponential way of finding positive wealth. Wealth in the form of great minds, joint ideas and decision making is always involved, and this is key.

Some people argue that wealth can be 'handed down.' Saying this to indicate that wealth can be handed down in terms of inheritance. My grandma often warned me that: 'So it comes, so it goes.' And grandma would constantly remind me that: "you can't take it with you."

In many cases, inherited forms of wealth don't seem to last. If wealth is 'handed down' to someone or inherited by an individual who is not prepared for it, they tend to 'go wild,' especially without the right guidance. For this reason, I say that some value of wealth ought to be within you. Your mind needs to be developed. Your thinking needs to be on another level.

You need to have an understanding that enables you to manage and maintain your wealth files to the degree that you will be able to access it. You need to know what to do in the event you need to process or access these Wealth files, for any reason. Wealth files are very important in the form of inheritance. As it becomes in line with your mindset, you are better able to manage them.

Wealth is commonly created in many millionaire-mindset types of people. Many wealthy people are often being created at first-generational levels too. In my environment today, and as this book is being written, several youngsters are using social media, and digital marketing, to create huge levels of wealth. They are accessing and creating wealth through different means of social activities. They are making use of the access to different technological advancements available to date.

While some people's wealth files may be at lower levels, the wealth files which you need to hold within yourself are very highly valued. Note this fact; your 'network' is equally impacting on your 'net worth.' How valuable your wealth files are may be closely related to your chosen 'circle of influence', and this being your valuable source of wealth.

THE CREATION OF HABITS

I mentioned earlier about your reasons why. Why you need to have habits and how using motion is a huge access point for this. Motion is a necessary avenue for habit creation. In your daily tasks, you create natural habits. Whether it be moving your limbs or your muscles, you create simple habits. Yes, even simply through walking and taking specific paths.

Wealth Creation Habits

When you follow a fashion or adopt a style, you can create a habit. The very track you walk and the path you use every day creates another sense of natural habit. You are creating habits, especially by the means of transport that you take regularly. Habits have a way of helping to energise you. Consider this the next time you take a casual walk, or a 'go get some air' type of stroll.

When you create habits, you create motion. When this motion is maintained, continuously, it tends to build on the initial stages. You advance from where you once were. As a result, your energy levels will be increased through the creation of such habits. You tend to build on what you initially created or where you first started. Having consistent effort and consistent actions contributes significantly to the creation of habits.

The creation of habits should be intentional. Over time you will struggle with creating habits. The struggle is because you have so many habits that you follow. Habits that you may have developed unconsciously. As a result, you may be consciously trying to break some of them. Habits will change. Some habits will take on different formations. It can seem senseless to think that you can easily change.

Creating a habit takes time and effort. So, how will you manage to somehow 'break your habit, overnight?' How will you do this in a very short period? In fact, why would you consider this? My grandma would remind me: 'Rome wasn't built in a day.' I had to figure this out my way to understand it. I learnt that many times during the process of creating a habit, you might need to break a pattern of activities, 'little by little.'

Your patterning of living your daily life tasks tends to take forms that are not always productive. If you are creating a habit through the process of changing or 'dropping' one habit, then it means that you need to replace that habit altogether. You will need to substitute that habit which you are looking to break, The habit which you are hoping to change. In order to replace or substitute for what is lacking and what's missing, you need to create a new habit.

When I reflect on my grandma's daily routine, I smile. At times some of the processes and practises in the mornings, especially while creating and developing a habit. It often seems a very positive experience as I recall her smiles after her prayer and meditation sessions. It seemed a great feat, as my grandma declared to: 'start your mornings right!'

Creating a habit will take time to develop. Creation of habits helps to keep you focused. It helps keep you on one path. The process keeps in an updated flow, what I referred to earlier, in productive 'wealth files. These packets of information within yourself are constantly being built on. They are constantly being improved. Yes, creating habits improves your wealth and success files altogether.

Remember too that reading tends to strengthen and build on your habits. Reading materials that relate to that habitual area or aspect of our life keeps a flow. While creating habits may energise you, in the same way, creating bad habits will mostly drain the energy from you. If built or created with consistent effort, a habit will remain with you consciously or unconsciously.

WHAT WEALTHY PEOPLE DO

What wealthy people do, relates to habits, as I have been banging on about, previously. Wealthy people do simple things. They do simple things in the sense where they're not complicated daily practices or tasks. Recently, I was reminded by one of my influences, Robert Kiyosaki's pieces, he said he maintains this simplicity idea. Robert and his wife, Kim Kiyosaki, indicated how they maintain their practice of a K-I-S-S system. They both indicated how their K-I-S-S, (kiss) system, meaning to keep-it-super-simple, is key to 'making them profits.'

Robert realised and indicated too how they leave behind, their previous experiences and some of their previous practices. He endured and experienced what it was like to be in a position where wealth would become overwhelming. Robert indicated how, while he learned that living a wealthy life had its rewards. He further learnt to simplify the things that he and his wife, Kim, do and now that makes them wealthier, while helping others in the process.

Another thing that wealthy people do is they have many access points. They have various modes of getting things done. Very often, wealthy people have access to different aspects of their life through multiple means. They tend not to take more time than is necessary to get tasks done. This realisation often takes me back to my grandma's casual warning: 'don't put off for tomorrow what you can get done today!'

Wealthy people specialise, and they stay focused. They focus on things that inspire and enlighten them, only things that lift them as individuals. Wealthy people tend to outsource or pass on responsibilities to other experienced professionals. Outsourcing saves them time so that they can do the tasks that they enjoy, and that they love. These are things that lift and energises you.

I can tell you from my experiences; wealthy people make a massive impact on other people's lives. Whether it be a business association or within a business environment, wealthy people take the time to surround themselves with like-minded individuals. They influence these individuals, and this is reciprocated in some way. Wealthy people like to engage in activities that create huge results, so they choose these energising settings.

When I recall how dedicated a person my grandma was, I often compare what I see in many of my experiences. Wealthy people help charitable organisations and support charitable work. They support several worthy causes. It is one major benefit of being wealthy as you can make a huge difference.

Being super rich allows for wealthy choices. Wealthy people live lifestyles that continue to be influential and impactful. It seems very difficult for them to put their work, their desires and their interests at rest. Wealthy people love money. They're not afraid to say that they love money because of what money can do and how money can make a huge impact on society and lives.

Do you feel uncomfortable with the thought of money? Are you comfortable to declare your love for wealth, money or riches? Why not read on and let us explore this more together.

MAKING AND BREAKING A HABIT

Wealthy people seem to synchronise their efforts. They seem to link their patterns of living with their lifestyle. Wealthy people like to create an impression, in whatever they do, they will systemise their efforts. This system is done in such a way to help break their habits They replace it with another similar and valuable activity. I admire how they can switch their drinking with say, smoking habits, in the name of health. This compared to their choices of preferred sporting activities.

While there are arguments and continuous discussion about habits, making a habit starts with simple effort. A simple recurring task, daily. In one of my programmes, I encouraged you to start habitual experiences with 15 minutes per day efforts. I like to indicate that if you can cover seven days consistently, you are on the way to starting a new habit or breaking a habit that you want to be rid of.

After seven days, if you can be consistent, you will need to focus on the next seven days. After these two seven-day periods, it becomes challenging to get through the next, and the last seven-day period, to embrace the changes. After three consecutive seven days of performing one activity, your natural behaviour, your natural sense of effort, will have been created. And so, after twenty-one (21) days a habit is being formed if there is unchanging behaviours or activities on a set task.

Twenty-one days (21) days is my indication of how to start creating a habit. Your activity will need to be consistent for the full twenty-one days. One of the strongest arguments, I've acknowledged remains ongoing, I will agree and indicate that three months is necessary for you to have a new habit fully developed. Equally, I will maintain that 21 days of one consistent activity, can work to change a habit.

One task, focused upon for 21 days, will put you on track to developing a new habit, and this comes from my experiences. So, if you can break a habit effectively, then I am sure you can replace a habit. With a practice of 21 days' consistent effort, then this must be a good start, if you're up for the challenge. In any positive task, you will benefit, as this involves growth.

Breaking a habit can be sealed and replaced after 21 days' continuous effort. While on your path, why not take this challenge, today? Yes! Why not try this today? Reach out to me. Let me know what your experience has been. Let me know how I can help you with this. I insist you do this: create a new habit with 21 days of consistent effort and consistent tasks.

Aspire As My Grandma Would Say

It is important here to remember that after seven days, if you have broken any pattern or day of activity of that task, you need to start all over again. After two weeks, yes. Even, say two consistent seven-day periods, you also need to restart, once you break the regular pattern. You must have a consistent period of 21 days to effectively break or make, if you are creating this new habit. You will need the full twenty-one (21) days to put that seal on it.

Notes

"Thinking expansively includes seeing what is possible and making it happen"
—(President) Donald J Trump

www.asmygrandmawouldsay.com

CHAPTER SIX

RICH THINKING ATTITUDES

THE RIGHT ATTITUDES

Having the right attitude is closely related to your being happy. Your happiness shows. Are you smiling? Why? Your happiness rests in your stories and your experiences. It is in what you emit to your world around you. This happiness comes from within. Having the right attitude creates a sense of happiness and invigorates energy. A happiness inclination within yourself tends to flow. It flows in such a way that when someone else sees you, you clearly show a sign of energy, within you.

A sign of brightness and a sense of jubilation in such a visual manner is reflected when you display the right attitude. Having the right attitude makes you appear to shine. As my grandmother would say: 'it's the glory of God.' Grandma had an amusing side to her, and it showed if you were lucky enough to experience it with her.

It's as if having the right attitudes takes you on a higher height. It takes you in a lofty place, as if you are floating on clouds. Have you ever felt this much happiness before? It makes you feel elated. Yes! Having the right attitude can make you feel like you're a light glowing or shining.

Having the right attitude liberates your mind. It releases your own feeling and your own sense of being. When you're happy, there's a sense of freedom within yourself. It's as if you can glide and as if you can feel or sense a smooth, warm flow of peace. A tender feeling within yourself. Do you know what I am talking about? How happy have you felt? What was your attitude like, then?

Another good thing about having the right attitude is it gives you that sense of being a problem solver for other people. Having the right attitude allows you to give advice. You tend to be in a supporting mood at times. It attracts others to come to you. You become a problem solver. Other people tend to lean towards you because of what they see and can sense, because of what you emit.

It's like you are expressing this 'good vibe' because of what you express. I am smiling as I write this as I am having some Rich thinking attitude right now. Do you have the right attitude for your success and your aspirations?

Having the right attitude is healthy. While you enjoy a sense of liberation or freedom within your mind or yourself, you tend to shine. You tend to feel and share happiness. If you're in good company, if you're in the right company of others, you'll have a vibe, and this too is your sense of happiness. It is coming from having the right attitude, and it deflects negativity. It deflects negative people, and it attracts instead, others that want to feel happy as well.

When other people who feel happy are attracted to you, they want to come within your environment. They want to be in your midst. They too increase your happy feeling and your happy energies. Having the right attitude will liberate you.

Rich Thinking Attitudes

RICHER THINKING

Think big! Like huge thoughts. Have better thoughts! This was the typical advice I had growing up. At least what I heard from my grandma's circle of influence and environment. Perhaps it's not the things you hear many older people say today. However, many people that I grew up around seemed to have had this instilled in their heads. In their minds, and within themselves, they heard this. Think big seemed 'the in thing' back then, yet it did not seem huge enough.

Having huge thoughts and of great quality is 'richer thinking.' I adopted this 'rich thinking' attitude through a series of personal development training and leadership affiliations. This thinking continued to be a significant element of my growth and in my achievements. More affluent people always think bigger. They think big because they have that mindset. They think big and have bigger thoughts because they want to achieve more.

Thinking big is a key part of their achievement. Why not make it yours too? Consider a small business owner. Imagine how they feel, the sense of importance. If you are a sole trader or a small business owner, then you're at this level. You can enjoy a sense of importance.

Of all the wealthy people that I've met, most of them think bigger. I've been learning about their 'how-to' as well. They might choose to be part of a group of small businesses, or they may have a chain of small business enterprises they own. They want to achieve more. They think bigger than the ordinary small-minded people do. Are you 'small-minded?' Do you feel comfortable thinking big, success levels?

As my grandma would often say, and I believe you need to do this too. Grandma would insist: 'think of serving others, as it gives you a sense of feeling fulfilled. It gives you another sense of importance to know that you have made a positive contribution.' I realised later how much you feel in a better place after you contribute to others. When you think more prosperous thoughts, you are creating a healthier state of mind for yourself too. And richer thinking is developed because you want to be effective and affect your world, positively.

Richer thinking allows you to add more value. It allows you to add value to others, and this affects different aspects of the world around you. When you think big, you achieve big. So why not have richer thinking? Your targets and you tend to grow bigger. Rich people thinking has influenced my mind-set to the extent where I continue to add value to others. As I think at higher levels, I have bigger and richer impacting results.

I am sharing with you to be a contributor to this world. To affect different aspects of this world, you too need to think big. Have more impactful thoughts. Have richer thinking attitudes. If you're a small business owner, it may give you a better sense of feeling, and help you realise your purpose. It may even impact on your sense of importance.

Whatever you choose, remember that thinking bigger or having richer thinking is another step to that elevation that you need to be more influential. Richer thinking will add to your feelings of a wealthy mind. It will add to your own achievements as you develop higher valued thoughts. You need to start using richer thinking.

Richer thinking is about having an effect and creating improved value. It is about having a much better result and having a more substantial influence. This influence will be more compact, and it will add value to others. You will contribute to other people's lives. You will contribute positively to your own rich thinking attitude.

Rich Thinking Attitudes

THE RICH WAYS TO HEALTH

I have not yet met anyone I can consider rich who does not think about their health. Neither have I learnt of anyone who is rich and who does not think that health is important. And so, I realised that rich people tend to have a way of life. Although they may be of huge influence, they tend to like sharing.

Most of the rich people that I am familiar with like to give back to society. They like to give back to others that's less fortunate, or that's lesser off. Note though, they don't want to support or promote the idea of 'handouts.' They do this via gift-giving and in their own methods. They share via their own charitable organisations.

Many rich people share by contributing to and supporting other charitable agencies and organisations. This support gives them a feeling of inner peace and is a rich way of being healthy. They think that they must help the less fortunate. They think that they must help others who have that desire to achieve. There are some people who, for some reason, whether it be poverty or lack of opportunities, they too want to achieve but are unable to. There are groups of Rich people who would reach out to them in different ways.

Various rich people tend to share their gifts, their wealth, and their talents, for 'just causes.' This action gives them a sense of fulfilment. It makes them feel a sense of well-being. Rich ways to health include looking after yourself. The rich style of living includes regular exercise, and today there is a massive shift to being healthier. It's as if eating foods that contain more nutrients has become a new phenomenon. Even exercising routines are becoming more popular.

Another way the rich look at their health is they take time out to rest. I was fascinated at the very way they take naps or siestas. They tend to get a good number of hours rest and sleep daily. This habit made me reflect on my grandma's habitual resting patterns. Even though her schedule seemed quite busy, grandma would take time out to rest and rejuvenate. She would have some 'switch off' periods when she'd say: 'child, let me rest my old bones.'

Similarly, even as some wealthy people become busy, they too have short periods to take a time out to rest, and to meditate. They allow their minds to exercise peacefully during periods of mediation and to regain inner strength. I've learned that as you become rich, you tend to look after your mind more. You tend to look after your most important asset and consider periods of rest as necessary. Recuperation becomes of vital importance.

In addition to regular exercise, the rich ways to health seem to include membership in clubs. They tend to belong to sporting groups, sporting organisations. The idea I've learnt is to have access to where they meet others that think on their same level. Where they can share in their ways and their ideas of healthiness, they congregate as a healthy way of life. What about you? What can you identify with here?

HEALTHY THINKING

Healthy thinking is inclined to that of a focused thinking. By focusing more and thinking more consciously, you tend to allow the mind to take a more natural course of developed action. Your focusing will enable the mind to work under less stress. It allows for thoughts to flow more peacefully, more calmly. Taking responsibility for your actions is essential when it comes to healthy thinking and helps to alleviate stress levels. It allows you to focus more gracefully. It will allow you to concentrate on what you must do.

Rich Thinking Attitudes

When you take responsibility for your own actions, you're able to look after your own mind. Avoiding negativity and creating a positive mindset allows you to be in a better position to help others. As part of your healthy thinking, the more people you help, the better your thoughts flow. Your thought process elevates at a higher level when in a positive state. As you look after your own mind, you will create a sense of positive awareness. You can then share and expand this in your immediate surroundings and your circle of influence.

The actions you take from your thinking can create a healthy, mindful environment. You can create this environment and include any structures you desire. When you choose to take time out to rest and to meditate, you can focus your thoughts. During these periods of rest, relaxation and meditation, you may decide to picture different environments and desired settings.

I sometimes take time out during my reflections and visualisations to visit the Caribbean. To visit and have a view of the beautiful sunny horizon over the ocean. To listen to the receding action of water on the seashores and feel the sea breeze as the wind massages my face and cheeks. It makes me smile and changes my mood altogether, no matter what my situation may be.

As my grandma would say: 'you are experiencing peace.' I realised later that this was a doorway to your spiritual connection. I like to refer to this experience as humbleness and tranquillity at times. As you relax and visualise, your thoughts and your focus actions take effect. This relaxation can produce pathways for more specific action steps.

An alternative to what seems like simply thinking about holiday spots, you can invest time in thinking about a clean and refined feeling in the environment. I will suggest learning to create a type of atmosphere you want. Can you imagine being in a place that makes you smile? For example, I like that feeling when I visualise the way I saw my grandma, as she sat and looked over the ocean in a very peaceful, calm, and fully-focused posture. I will observe my grandma during her periods of silence.

My grandma would say nothing during those periods of contemplation and relaxations. I recognised that she was connected with her healthy state of mind. I learned how grandma would be looking at her surroundings and elevating her mind as she reflected on past experiences and achievements. Grandma will reflect on the influences she's had in her community, and she will look at me with a stare. It was as if to show me her path, in her eyes. Then she would look away expressionless, as if to say: 'you are not yet ready.'

Healthy thinking is helpful thinking. As you grow in thoughts, you grow in influence, and you grow in focus. This healthy thinking must take effect consciously, as a reflective activity and as a pre-planning action. To think is to grow. To grow is to develop more structured thoughts. Are you having healthy time, regularly?

WEALTHY THINKING

When I explained how the rich think compared to that of the wealthy, Robert Kiyosaki comes to mind. Robert Kiyosaki in his 'Rich Dad, Poor Dad' series has been echoing this for several years. He outlined different structures and aspects of where the wealth in many environments resides. Wealthy thinkers think with a specific mindset. They seem to systemise everything.

In fact, anything the wealthy can systemise; they tend to create a structure and then put the necessary things in place. They want to automate the system or have the system running as effectively and efficiently as possible. Wealthy thinking involves the idea of legacy.

Rich Thinking Attitudes

As my grandma would say: 'think of how it would have an effect.' Wealthy thinkers tend to have an attitude of wealth-sharing. They want to share their wealth. They want to share their skills, and they want to share how they made their wealth. The wealthy thinkers want to go out on a quest to share and teach different skills that show that it's possible.

Wealthy thinkers show how you can gain knowledge and create wealth in different ways for yourself too. In the same way, you may engage in apprenticeships with them. Others may create workshops that tend to spread their knowledge in different groups. Their passion tends to be in helping more and more people to achieve. They encourage you to connect with the right thought process, and you learn how to think 'wealth.'

Wealthy thinking does include a skill set of which a huge part of this includes confidence building. Wealthy thinking tends to be firm and taking command. This thinking tends to involve a sense of influence. To affect more and more lives, you must be influential. Wealthy thinking involves the creation of wealth, and a significant part of that is in the thought process.

Again, Robert Kiyosaki, in his 'Rich Dad Poor Dad' series, has been outlining how the education system has failed. Robert explains how for so many years, there's been alternative ways of teaching, learning, and educating in order to help the vast majority. His ideas have gone on to help larger communities to think on a larger scale. He is teaching how to think on a wealthy and highly influential level.

WHY DO THE RICH THINK BIG?

There are different categories of rich people. Several of whom I met have shared similar views, and a few have shared different principles. Most of them, however, despite various principles, do share similar aspects of why they think big. Rich people don't want to be broke. They can't stand the thought or idea of being less off in the position they are today.

There have been times when I like to refer to one of the stories of the USA (President) Donald Trump. At times you'll hear that while a billionaire, he was broke and in a very short time was able to get back to his status. The rich think big because they have a mindset that keeps them elevated. This mindset relates to their actions and ability. Their thoughts elevate them to higher heights. They think big because they want to succeed.

To succeed, you need to have the right mentality. You need that thought process of wanting to elevate yourself. You must have that desire of wanting to succeed. You must have that desire to achieve something big. You must think big!

T. Harv Eker often shares the idea of having a financial blueprint. He indicates in several of his teachings that rich people have a financial blueprint in their minds. Their systems and mindset, is where they operate from. Because of this financial blueprint, the rich can maintain their status. This blueprint benefits them mentally and physically as a result. What is your financial blueprint? Do you know why you think the way that you do?

Robert Kiyosaki sometimes mentions the idea of being a visionary. I embrace this quality, and I believe it will benefit you similarly. Robert is known for this aspect of his skillset and shares it in his 'Rich Dad, Poor Dad' series and most of his books. Robert Kiyosaki repeats his instructions in most of his teachings and he refers many years of predictions. He has proved many financial results in various markets. In different countries, Robert has proved to be quite accurate. How big do you think?

My grandma had her own idea about riches. I often reflect on the fact that my grandma did think big. I also like to consider that, particularly, after her death, my grandma left tangible proof of her riches. This became more evident in what she left behind in the form of property of various values. As I observe my family turn some of this property into meaningful, profitable, and rewarding wealth.

I will recall my grandma's wealth status as social proof of her thinking big and her way of thinking big went beyond her personal benefit. It reminded me of the whole idea of T. Harv Eker's financial blueprint.

Thinking big creates big results. If you don't think big and have a normal practice of thinking at small levels, then this will be your results. Being a small thinker tends to be your restriction. This type of thinking limits your level of expertise and automatically creates small results. Whatever you choose today, choose to go big! Think big as the rich do, and see your big results follow you too.

BRANDING YOUR VIEWS

Your system, your name, your company, all belongs to you. While being recognised for this is a personal choice, these aspects of you, do represent you. They are some of the things you want to consider if you want to be unique. You can be identified for this and for being original. Your views, your ideas, your systems can all be branded. The rich and successful people sometimes suggest branding as a necessary area for you to be distinct.

You too, can be or have a recognised brand. Whether it be your views or your ideas, this can be done in various forms. You can brand your views as a part of a business. Today, at this time of writing, you can 'brand' your views and ideas as an individual or as a company, altogether. You may have a company name or an idea in your head that you want to make public in a structural form. Why not become a reality at some point? Why not make it real, for example, in the form of your intellectual property.

By branding your idea in the form of a company, you remain original. As a business, you could be identified for what you are, what you do, and what you stand for, in different ways. You may want to brand your views by name in the form of your name. It is advisable and some professionals have been doing this for some time now. Especially if you want to be identified by your name and your profession and how you influence others.

You may choose to brand your name as a professional speaker, a trainer, or another professional, let's say, as a consultant. Sometimes you see some big businesses, some unique professions, and even companies, use a personal name as their brand. As a personal identity, practical examples include: 'Oprah,' (Oprah Winfrey), 'Les Browne' (Leslie brown) and 'Trump' (USA, President, Donald Trump).

While speaking about 'branding your views,' the rich thinking attitude comes to mind. Robert Kiyosaki comes up often as he has a distinct branding of 'Rich Dad (Poor Dad)' materials. Again, (President) Donald Trump, with his Trump Enterprise and his Trump name – a very expensive name today. He is quite a unique example of branding your name and creating your own identity and in branding your views. Both Robert and President Trump are individual authors, as well.

Another thing which is becoming more prevalent and popular in some industries; especially in training, is the 'speaking industry.' People are branding their 'intellectual property. You can do this with ideas and tools which are developed in the form of books, other training materials, and different types of publications. Intellectual property is being stepped up in a variety of effective systems as well. What sort of intellectual property will you like to explore?

Branding your views is becoming more popular today. You may be able to brand your views in different forms. Your focus, your intentions and your system of doing things, they're all your views. Your ideas, and perhaps your passion, can be tools you will use to enhance someone's life. You can be branding these aspects of you. Branding your views will help bring you in line with the thinking and attitudes of the rich and wealthy.

Other successful people, some trainers, coaches and thought-provoking individuals, started with a simple idea. As my grandma would say: 'In whatever you do, make a difference in people's lives. How will you use your influence? How will you use your 'know-how' for a 'just cause?'

THINKING BIG

Rich thinking attitudes focus on several wealthy practices, among them 'thinking big' is often common. As T. Harv Eker mentions, having a financial blueprint is important in plotting your financial future. Your level of thinking and your thought processes need to be on a specific level to succeed. Similarly, to the wealthy or rich person, your success becomes bigger as they think bigger.

You must be able to think bigger than yourself. Thinking big can move you in different ways and this may include spiritually or emotionally. However, whether it be mentally, psychologically or physically, you will have an internal shift of different levels. Success starts with a thought process, and in thinking big, you're rewarded for exercising your thinking. Exercising the use of your brain, and looking after your appearance, can reflect your thinking levels. You tend to develop a new form of posture, both mentally and physically. You will develop a different way of doing things overall.

When you think big, you tend to see more and more opportunities. You will visualise and increase your mental capacity. Your brain tends to act, and you go into your 'flow' as your potential for growth is being triggered. Being a risk-taker will become more prevalent. Taking educated risks starts with thinking big and particularly thinking bigger than yourself. So, when you think big and focus away from yourselves, yes!, your mind goes into action and your thought process elevates you.

As I reflect on my earlier ventures in the network marketing industry, I remember an experience I had where I began to expand territories in my mind. As I started in one country and began to elevate my thinking, I realised that I was reaching out to, too many people in my community. It was as if I started to find myself connecting with different clans. I had this drive within myself where I was reaching out to friends, family, then expanding my dimension in other countries. For this reason, I was able to travel more.

I had a new purpose in my mind, and my thought process was extending. I was able to meet and reconnect with others that I had not seen or spoken to for long periods. My mindset has changed and yours will change too. Your thought process will expand as you develop from your own exercising of the mind. When you start thinking bigger than yourself, you will find ways and reasons to reward yourself in different ways. There is ongoing research, and there are facts that indicate that thinking big is connected to your success.

I can reference individuals like Robert Kiyosaki and his education system. In his cashflow games, Robert introduces his financial education and training. Another legend: T. Harv Eker,

Rich Thinking Attitudes

whom I have become very familiar with, emphasises his teaching on financial mindsets and shows you how to connect this with being happy. T. Harv has indicated the use of affirmations and declarations in your thought process to help you move from where you are now in your thinking. Using affirmations and declarations has enabled me to think bigger than myself, creating a new mindset and a different way of thinking.

As I continue to change and map a better journey, I'll like you to challenge yourself. Why not examine and evaluate yourself? Ask yourself the question: ''where am I today?' and, 'How big are my thoughts?'

Aspire As My Grandma Would Say

Notes

"Be grateful for all that you have, accepting of all that you don't, and actively create all that you want."
—Hal Elrod

CHAPTER SEVEN
SPIRITUALITY AND RICHES

SPIRITUAL THINKING

When you're a spiritually inclined person, you tend to engage in practices of deep thought, and in medication, and visualisation. You will tend to be in a controlled environment within your mind. You will feel elevated within your thoughts, and your way of life will seem 'different.' Spiritual thinking does involve the freedom to move much freely. Whether you think psychologically or in your head, i.e., 'in your mind,' as some people refer to it, you tend to move and think way beyond the norm.

During periods of visualisations, you can exercise your journeys. You can mentally create experiences of going way beyond where you are now. You can travel back and forth into your present. Yes, go into your past at times, and even into your future. Your spiritual thinking will allow you to lift your limitations. You tend to think beyond yourself and defy your limitations. You are elevated, and this could be, beyond your expectations. Spiritual thinking is a possible experience when you practice and live as a spiritual being.

Aspire As My Grandma Would Say

Spiritual thinking is a practice that may sometimes get attached, solely to a religious person or a deity. For me, the way that my grandma taught me is that spiritual thinking is part of you and closely related to your prayer life experiences. You can have your personal, deep thoughts, and your own connections with your higher being.

You may not believe at times that an inner being and a higher being does exist. Some people may declare their love for their higher power and their beliefs. Either way, your own experiences in having this type of experience, or this way of life, is real.

I have found spiritual thinking quite deeply linked to mindfulness. Both spirituality and 'meditative practices' as I'll say in the lesser sense, are real to me. When I practice my meditation routines, I tend to look deep within myself, and this helps me to visualise more clearly. I am then able to envision tasks and activities which I intend to achieve today and beyond. What about you? What is your spiritual thinking like? Why not take a moment to reflect on your thoughts before you move on?

THE RICH MENTALITY

When I became familiar with the story around the *'untethered soul,'* it reminded me of my earlier practices and a belief that was entwined within me. Surprisingly, I later became interested with a book with a similar title, by Michael A. Singer. This interest occurred through my continued coaching and learning. As I learn more about rich and wealthy people, I often compare the qualities of other successful people.

There are many similarities, as well as some identifiable differences among the titled: 'rich—wealthy and successful.' I continue to learn more and more about giving of yourself. You may

Spirituality And Riches

want to donate to charity, help other people, or give of yourself. It has become a harsh reality that you must look after yourself, first. I have learnt and experienced that when you have succeeded or elevated at a higher level, you become more useful and more capable of giving.

As I meet and become familiar with the rich, and the wealthy, I become more familiar with this harsh reality. I've come to realise that despite your achievements, you need to accept that you are now in a better place and a healthier mental state. Your achievement will allow you to decide who and how you want to give to charities and other 'just causes.'

I once established a thought in the past that 'riches and wealth' are of 'no great use to you' unless it is used for a greater good. There's always a need for replenishment too. Rich people, and perhaps you too, may associate the rich here with successful people. Have you ever considered this particular reason why? As well as thinking alike, they tend to be sharers of wealth. Successful and rich mentality involves the need for sharing, for giving, and for helping.

Additionally, having the rich mentality lifestyle seems to include fulfilment, a connection with the art of meditation and a spiritual nature. These tend to be common practices in daily routines. I have had discussions and other non-intentional conversations with successful people. Their idea around the topic of spirituality seems to connect as they share it, and this tends to be different in several ways.

A rich and successful mentality differentiates that spirituality is not subject to any denominations, any specific spiritual beliefs or any religious system or organisation. As my grandma would say: 'what is riches if you can't live to enjoy it. 'The rich mentality is one that is filled with giving and one that believes in 'beyond yourself.'

Your idea as you aspire and achieve needs to develop the principle in sharing of wealth, of riches, and in helping others, this is the rich mentality.

ARE RICH PEOPLE SPIRITUAL?

I would be doing a massive injustice if I stated here that all rich people are spiritual. What I do know is that there are some levels of commonality. Some of the rich, the wealthy, other successful people and some of the great achievers have several similarities. The ones that I've read and learned about in different ways are mostly of a 'humble' attitude. Some I've met seem humbled at different times in their achievements; by something or by someone that has impacted on their life.

I can say too that all rich people practice having periods of silence and believe in something beyond themselves. This is not to say that all rich people are spiritual. Your own understanding, your own growth and extended belief may doubt the fact that you can be rich and spiritual. Rich people, whether they're atheists or of religious beliefs or backgrounds do have the belief in an energy within.

Whether the belief is deep within themselves that they alone can control. They believe that they can achieve. They believe they can do whatever is necessary or whatever is possible. This is a belief system within itself. What about you? What do you believe? I have met several atheists, and I've seen converts who now share the wealth and who share riches.

Similarly, I've met and had interactions with past atheists who may not believe in one God and may have rejected the idea of spirituality. They may share a belief in a higher being. They may have had faith in themselves and faith in other people, or in their workmate who they find a connection with. They have voiced that they may have faith in what they do to succeed at it.

There are some rich people that I've become aware of who believe in connecting with their spiritual energy. They believe something exists in the atmosphere, in the 'ether.' This energy has been described in many forms. One of the earlier influences in personal development and success thinking, Napoleon Hill, has spoken many times about ether and the energies that exist. Napoleon Hill has shared in many ways of how the ether can work in your favour.

I too, have tried and later connected with this concept of ether. Hill has delved deeply into thoughts and the airwaves. He has thought of the connections with others in spiritual ways. This concept further helped me better understand the idea of 'masterminding.' Dale Carnegie, another thought leader and founder in many of our industries, alluded this belief in a higher power and outer energies. He has stated too how this energy helps to propel you. And how it motivates your drive toward achieving ultimate successes.

This energy is not to be misunderstood with that of what our bodies generate—the food we eat, your drinks, and our intake of nutritional items. Rich people have their spiritual exercises or spiritual practices. They are of various forms however they do exist.

MEDITATIVE APPROACH

My grandma has continued with her ancestral links, from a generation of contemplatives, of Christianity, and similar beliefs and practices. As a result, I grew up having been close-knit with her and learning about spirituality. I have grown to accept and learn of deep belief, of prayer and its power. In learning about prayer and the 'power' of prayer, I grew to have several experiences that have taken me to my knees and taught me more about humbleness.

My experiences have connected me with other religious leaders. I have met other spiritual people who have had their personal experiences that I can say I do identify with. My experiences have taken me a long way to accept and learn to believe in what seems like the supernatural. It has been a long journey, perhaps of faith and of prayer.

I identified something unique in my life journey, and it was related to the plotting and tracking of my different daily practices. In my own practising, of my own 'Life S.E.R.V.A.S (or →S.A.V.R.E.S), as recognised by Hal Elrod's: Life [S.A.V.E.R.S]. It was through a process of being coached and in coaching other individuals that I've learned of others' beliefs too. My journey connected me to others' belief systems and mechanisms.

After connecting with the 'Miracle Morning' community, and other enthusiasts, I have looked at my practices and reviewed the plotting of my life journey. As I saw the huge similarity with Hal Elrod's ideas in the 'Miracle Morning' I was able to embrace better how I started the day. Hal revealed a very important and amazing point in stating that many successful people practise at least one element of the Life S.A.V.E.R.S at the start of their day.

I have been following my own practises for several years before now connecting with thousands of others. As I have now gained greater awareness, I continue to redefine and make changes. I am now committed to a 'meditative approach' to the start of my days. First thing in the morning, or at least at the beginning of my days, I start my days in a 'better state of mind.' I have a huge energy level when I start my day right.

As a result of Hal Elrod's life-SAVERS, I too practice my methods and with greater enthusiasm. My system (my life-S.E.R.V.A.S) which very much exemplifies Hal Elrod's own experiences have gained momentum, and it works. Over the years, I have practised these in several different ways. Connecting with Hal Elrod's own 'meditative approach' seems to propel me even more as I identify with him and many of his teachings.

Through contemplation, meditation practises, and the power of affirmations, I have been able to propel my start to the day. And so, as you set off on your day, you can have a more energised morning period. You can now start your day with similar practices or concepts. Whether it's my or Hal Elrod's, this idea of a meditative approach needs to include your own style. You too can select your elements for a similar more energised 'miracle morning.'

I have adopted and practised a life of deep contemplativeness. My spiritual beliefs, and what I have seen and experienced through the power of prayer, I now know. Now it's your turn. Whether it's your belief in a higher being, your relationship with your God can be phenomenal experience in your meditative approach.

The power of congregations and people joining or coming together for one cause is powerful. Focusing and praying and supporting each other in your own beliefs has its own greatness in that meditative approach. A great part of your journey and continuing your day is affected by the start. The idea of a period for prayer or silence or meditation is in this 'meditative approach' which helps propel your day's activities.

RICH SPIRITUAL HABITS

Some practices are more inclined to be associated with the rich, the wealthy and the successful. Yet, not every habit that resonates with the rich is exclusive to these individuals. Some rich and spiritual habits can be more common than expected. You and I may have practised several of these, at some time. Some may even come from our own beliefs. Rich spiritual habits may include the simple habit of 'letting go of stuff.'

As we grow, as we develop and associate ourselves with different people and different environments, we tend to take upon ourselves the burden of other people's stresses, troubles and worries. This is a huge: No-No! Rich spiritual habits will not allow worrying, holding them down. They will not allow worrying or 'indecision' to hold them back from acting. So why should you, or me?

Rich spiritual habits is not one that lacks fear. Fear is within you and me in different ways. Fears can be seen and used as an energy driver. Sometimes you may look at having fears as a means of policing your ideas, and our thoughts. In comparison, rich spiritual habits involve consistent and deep focus thinking. In this process, when you meet your fears, you may develop a 'flight and fight' reaction.

Through deep thought and especially through the practice of consistent meditation, you can learn to see different perspectives. Coupled with the use of visualisation, you can tend to develop a feeling of wanting to be free. My grandma often reminded me that the only fear I should have is 'fear of God' and I have grown to ask the odd why questions. Perhaps it is because of my own experiences; I may have found the answers. 'What about you? What fears do you have? Are you willing and able to confront them?

Freedom, as I've learned, is free, but it does have a price. The fears that we have can sometimes hurt us. As such, you must face your fears. You need to develop methods of conquering these fears or managing them; this is not the same as avoiding fears. In your rich spiritual habits, you will tend to have consistent ways of dealing with and letting go of stuff. You will learn to face your fears.

Through consistent practises, you develop your habits, and this gives you that hunger and that need to feel free. Embracing your fears is a rich way of thinking. It helps in the habit of creating renewed energy. In fact, there are strong elements of spirituality when you commit to this habit.

MEDITATION AND RICHES

I have often found myself in the company of others asking the question: "What does meditation have to do with riches or successes?" Sometimes I smile at the answers, and partly because of my own experiences. It is interesting learning from my connections with wealthy and successful people. Many of them continue to teach me about their experiences. And somehow, they've used meditation to help them in their wealth creation. What I found most interesting is how important it is in their everyday practices.

I have mentioned previously how rich people tend to use meditation and visualisation as a daily practice. It's mostly a habit that they've developed, and it helps them to release. Releasing and 'letting go of' stuff tends to help you to free your mind and create mental space. You can free your whole being of things that perhaps are holding you back. To claim your riches, whether it be spiritual or financial; or whether it be other forms of wealth and success, you must learn to 'let go.' Let go of the things that are holding you back.

Release yourself, insist that you must learn to release any tensions. This release will help you create mental space, and meditation, and breathing exercises, helps a great deal. Connecting with your awareness and your inner being is one of the better practices I've found as invigorating. I believe that will help you as it focuses on creating the reality of 'wholeness.' Meditation has become an essential practice to connect with your inner being. It helps you to connect with you.

You will learn to release that pressure and that inner weight that tends to burn you out, especially with other people's stuff. Your day to day activities and stresses are enough to keep you busy. It is more than enough to occupy your mind and to block you from acquiring your own riches. When you decide to claim your riches, you will want to explore different activities. You will have different practices that you can use to help activate that inner strength.

That inner power that sometimes seems lacking can be realised as you meditate and create a clearer vision. As I recall my grandma's guidance, her actions, and as I feel her presence, I know how powerfully, and effective this action is. It's like saying it this simple. Meditation helps you connect with your higher power. You can reconnect you with that 'ether.' That invisible power that you communicate with and helps give you a sense of direction.

Although it may not seem real or practical in the first instance, rich and successful people tend to use meditation. Coupled with visualisation, it helps them to set goals. It develops them and releases certain energetic vibes. From my experience, it drives you as if to propel your impulses, your nerves, and your whole being. Meditation can help you create a sense of posture and a sense of readiness. You tend to realise a sense of unlimited energy levels. What are your thoughts on 'meditation?' Have you tried it yet?

MEDITATION AND MINDFULNESS

My first memories of meditation go back to me, observing my grandma during her praying sessions. I had negative thoughts then. Meditation as I recall and from my experience, is that practice of becoming more aware, and connecting with the centre of your awareness. During this action, through focused thoughts and focused thinking, there is a sense of energy that could be driven within yourself. Through the simple act of breathing and having the right posture, with the right focus, you can release.

The energy that you develop through simply breathing is one that helps your emotional structure, your mental state—your mindfulness. I observed my grandma in my early childhood, and now I am a believer. I have researched and continue to observe more ideas surrounding meditation and mindfulness. I know now that it helps in recreating a source of our unlimited energy. Mindfulness keeps you in that central awareness path, as you meditate. Why not try this now?

There are certain energies that you can develop, when you intentionally synchronise specific movements, as you breathe and as we move. Why not re-read the actions above and once you're in a safe space, try these actions. Often, these methods are associated with elements of the different art form, including Tai Chi, Yoga, Pilates, and other aerobic type exercises. Some of these practices and routines involve the use of focused thinking to help with your emotional state and awareness.

Centralising your thinking and remaining in the present within your thoughts does have a richness in how you develop your inner strength. Your focus, and your actions tend to connect. And meditation is practised in many forms. As I've experienced this over some years, I've realised the best practices must involve breathing. With the right use of your breath – inhaling, exhaling – this helps you to connect with your thoughts, much better.

As my grandma would say: 'connect with your spirit.' You too can connect with your meditation and be in that state of focused, central awareness, By closing your eyes, you can be connecting with your thoughts, much stronger. This tends to create a better sense of energy and an unlimited feeling of power within yourself. Please remember to ensure that it is safe before you carry out any of the above actions. You can 'reach out' for some guidance and to learn more about connecting with your mindfulness using mediation.

MONEY AND SPIRITUALITY

Have you ever noticed this on any television shows? That amongst various religions denominations and churches, how well dressed the pastors and preachers or ministers appear to be? Oh, how they look quite distinctly happy, wealthy, and well-kept.

I grew up in an environment that had mixed feelings and mixed beliefs around money. At different points growing up, I heard money does not grow on trees. I never actually heard this from my grandma, and I am glad I did not. I've heard things like money talks, and BS walks. I've heard other belief concepts and sayings, particularly, sayings that often do not connect money and spirituality in any way.

One of my grandma's sayings that she often repeated was: "Don't worry, God will provide." I often saw that sense of spirituality in her, and in her faith. I have seen a strong connection with her strengths and her belief in prayer. Sometimes I would say different in her midst to get some reaction. Other times I think I noticed little display of much food. Every time I asked where the food or groceries were, my grandma would tend to say, "Don't worry. God will provide." It did seem obvious at times, as I grew older.

I realised over time that being spiritually inclined has its merits. Being deep and a contemplative person who believes in prayer does not mean the absence of loving or wanting to gain more money.

Spirituality And Riches

Having money is a choice. Making money is a choice. Being poor or being rich is a choice. Money is a means to an end. It is part of the rewards aspect. Money is needed in any society to make things happen.

There are various levels and teachings of belief systems. Most times in Christianity, there is a saying that 'love of money is bad' or that money is 'the root of evils.' There have often been some misconceptions here too. In the church and the religious arena, I've questioned this phrase and 'saying' amongst the church and worship leaders. Different churchy-churchy enthusiasts often go on the defensive and become defensive. This has worried me.

I've asked the question around money and spirituality, and it's alluded me to even the life of Mother Theresa. Often, individuals and groups donated lump sums of monies. Many of these individuals came from various backgrounds. Mother Theresa, from what I've learned, would often seek to place a blessing on these funds and donations. She has allowed her donations to grow and help rebuild lives and communities.

Mother Theresa has gone on to help the needy, the poor, and help others in poverty-stricken environments. Point to note here is that Mother Theresa' commitments didn't necessarily stop her from living or enjoying some amenities in life. And I need not go into this. There have been a series of Q&A's around money and spirituality. What I do know is that what I've learnt and observed in different countries and different environments is interesting. Religious leaders can profit from their choice of livelihood and their vocation, in many cases.

Pastors, reverends and other church leaders don't often live for free. Many do not live an impoverished lifestyle either. Whatever your level of spirituality, money is needed to operate the church, money is necessary to run or for the upkeep of the relevant establishments and the places of worship. Money can cause the stirring and a series of confusions, if you allow for it. Many questions are raised because of this issue around money and spirituality. Consider what your views are on money and spirituality. Do you feel comfortable with this topic?

Notes

"You know more than you think you know"

—Andrew CM Miller

CHAPTER EIGHT
ASPIRING TO EXCEED

MY ASPIRATIONS TO EXCEED

As a child growing up, I was secretly competitive. Now, as I think of this, I laugh at the thought. Being secretly competitive and growing up in different environments had a wealth of experiences connected with my childhood. I grew up in different territories, and on different islands, in various locations. As a child, some of my memories include me spending a lot of time with family friends.

Growing up with friends, allowed me to experience being in the wild; the bushes, as it was often referred to. I spent time with friends rearing a range of animals. My childhood experiences had their spill offs too. My usual upbringing caused me to experience being in and out of different early years of schooling. My early stages of primary education had me moving forward and back at different stages of my classes.

I would say I grew up secretly competitive for various reasons. I often wanted to get the highest marks or highest grades. I wanted to win at times. I did not take part in a lot of activities, such as sports, during school, I did, however, have my playtime outside of school environments. I raced, I competed, and I had my youthful fights. And I always approved myself as the winner.

I did have my challenges for sure too. As I was often moving between different territories, some students did find the need to mock me or to put up an odd challenge. They seemed to make an example of me as if I was an 'odd figure.' In fact, they seemed to convince me at times that I didn't belong. Here on, I learned that when you are a visiting student or settling in a temporary school environment, you always seem to be the outsider. You either 'stand out' or you get 'found out!'

Have you ever had the experience of someone seeing you as different? Have you been classified as being unsociable? This experience is no different. If you can relate, then you will know this: it is a fact that every time you have a new experience or start something in a new environment, it takes time. And so, in school, I had to create my own 'flow.' Even though I learnt how to make friends easily, I didn't try to be popular with everyone. I was very selective in who became close to me.

I chose who I shared my inward feelings with. This behaviour continued for some time. It stayed with me into my young adult stages before I realised that I was not normal. I learned to accept that all through my childhood and school journeys, 'I was aspiring to exceed.' What I had seen as different or hard were challenges. My aspiration to exceed did not waiver.

I had the opportunity to study for several years in the USA. I attended a college, and I was not the brightest of students. I did, however, manage, and 'stood-out' in several things. I took the time-out and visited several States and provinces. I travelled to different countries until I emigrated to the United Kingdom. In London, I had a profound experience studying within the education system, even though most of the time, outside of the school environment.

Aspiring To Exceed

I was already in full-time employment when I decided on studying in the UK. My focus was hugely on business, and on exceeding and in being a leader. I had already developed many of these qualities within me. I maintained my aspirations, just as my grandma instilled in me from childhood.

ASPIRE TO ACHIEVE

For several years, I have been aspiring to achieve, as my grandma would say. Despite a series of experiences in the Caribbean, the US, and in the United Kingdom, I found recreating the best version of me. I have enjoyed experiences training and working with other individuals in areas such as Canada and other locations in Europe, while continuing my 'personal quest.' I have been aspiring to achieve through a series of exploring and connecting. I have been forming networks, connecting points, connecting people and connecting with like-minded individuals.

What about you? Why not explore some of your aspirations? What are some of your dream journeys?

At some stages of my schooling, I remember a period of being part of a student government body. I volunteered to act in some leadership positions. Although this seemed to give me that feeling of perhaps power, more so, I was able to serve even more effectively. I worked with other individuals for a higher cause. To have a positive impact is to have an influence that will make lasting changes. Doing this will be directly beneficial when it is done with specific aspirations at the core of your purposes.

When I engaged in student leadership, this gave me an opportunity to be able to travel widely. Travelling to different parts of countries allowed me to observe views of several different cultures. I can remember the sites as I was visiting places in the

USA such as Las Vegas, Detroit and Atlanta. It was exhilarating to identify locations like the MGM Grand that you usually see in films.

While visiting Detroit, Michigan, I observed locations where the GMC trucks were pioneered and were once very popular. When I visited places like Texas, I could identify and see the resemblance and with the cowboys-western stories. The cowboy hats and the distinctive boots did make me wonder about limiting beliefs and the idea of legends.

My early explorations and student leadership was only the start of a much more meaningful journey. Where I am here today is a very focused type working with businesses, working with families, and working with individuals. I assist in your process to transition from where you are today and where you want to get to. I have learnt how to help others to adjust their thought processes on pathways, Also, how to help them get on their pathways and maintain this toward their success.

I remember my grandma's encouragement, her teachings and her support systems. I reflect on how, by supporting me and allowing me to live freely, I was able to explore and see the bigger pictures of life. I learned to aspire to greatness and see beyond what physically was in and around my environment. I learned how to see beyond my physical location, to explore what seemed like a speck on the map.

What limiting conversations are you struggling with today? Why not consider something different for a moment. Can you relate to this?

I grew up in an early stage from a little speck of island in the Caribbean, called Canouan. Today I smile, and sometimes I laugh at the thought of my grandma's vision. She was an elderly lady who had not travelled out of her birth home and territory, yet she planted a seed 'within me' She instilled a seed for vision, filled with thoughts and wisdom. And so, I believe that this caused me to want to explore the adventure, to aspire and to achieve.

EXCEED YOUR KNOWLEDGE BASE

Although I can revel at the idea of travelling, exploring, visiting different countries, and different territories, this didn't give me the success that I needed or that I wanted. One of my mentors alluded to the fact that my income will not exceed my own level of thinking, my development personally or my knowledge base. This fact puzzled me a bit and seemed to give me that well needed 'wake-up call' on my journeys to success. In fact, on several occasions, I have questioned what I have learnt.

In the earlier stages of my involvement in network marketing, I would sit in presentations and workshops and look at the age differences of the audience or the next guy who was very successful. I often asked myself the same question repeatedly; "what's really different between me and him/her?" Apart from a few thousand sums of dollars ($), and later, pounds (£)!

I needed to rethink and revisit what I was doing daily and this helped raise my red flags to some extent. I started facing different challenges; financially and especially from restarting various ventures. My relationship break-ups and breakdowns, were drowning me. There came the point where I had to 'take stock.' I questioned myself and analysed when and where I was on my journey of aspiring to exceed.

As I think back on the idea of 'knowledge', The Knowledge Cube comes to mind. This concept I alluded to and expanded on as I shared the creation of an entire concept in my book, 'The

Knowledge Cube Concept.' I started connecting to the idea of the mastermind and connecting networks.

In creating your knowledge base and inspiring powerhouses, you can connect with like-minded people and solve more problems. You will learn how to bring people together, using your skills and your knowledge. Your 'know-how' will continue to expand your knowledge base. Despite my experiences, my learning and my training, I have been gaining experiences through different business ventures and different challenges. I needed to rethink.

It was in writing my book, that changed the standard of my knowledge base. Visiting and exploring what is inside of me and getting it out in the form of a publication, made me realise that I can exceed my knowledge base through several avenues. My book revelation, although years in the making, came to me through a series of network events, connecting with the right people, Other like-minded and successful personnel.

Why not question your actions and the avenues that you are using to expand and exceed your knowledge base?

HOW TO EXCEED EXPECTATIONS

My experience in network marketing and perhaps your experience in your early stages of business ventures and exploration in your expertise, would bring you to the point of creating your own vision. At some stage in your life, I would indicate that you take the time out to create and mould your vision within yourself. Although you want your vision to be seen externally, to shape or create a structure of what you want to achieve, you may need to create this in your mind's eye, firstly. In your own sense, you need to be able to picture your own vision while using your own form of activities.

Aspiring To Exceed

I suggest you look at your reason or reasons 'why' you're trying to achieve what you are currently pursuing. Your reason could be as simple as you trying to achieve that new bike, car. Or whether it's a new job or a new home, or to provide for your family. There is an ultimate driving force within you for that next thing in your life. Your reason 'why' needs to be strong enough that it appears to be on your mind, automatically. When you wake up in the morning, in the middle of the night, or paused for any odd reason during the day. The reason 'why' you want to do what it takes, no matter what. The reason 'why' you want to achieve your vision and to exceed your expectations.

It makes sense to know that if you are aspiring to exceed expectations, that you need to make room for what is to come your way. You can empty yourself of emotional burdens, in many forms—You can let go of your material possessions and pass them on. You can get rid of some things you don't need. Perhaps, change some of the things that you own. Spiritually, you can find within yourself that desire to give more of yourself and of what you do that is life-changing. You can give more of yourself to help others on their journey.

You may need to look inwardly and at yourself. Give yourself time to heal by investing in yourself and your 'self-care.' Allocate time to search and to do more for you. Find more of what you need for you. It is in giving more for you that you effectively exceed. Whether it be time for yourself to grow or to heal, give of your time to help others to achieve. It is in giving that you open the way and the path to receive what is coming towards you.

Exceeding expectations require that you are open to receiving. Be open to receiving gifts, awards, likes, dislikes and challenges. Be open to receiving conflicting ways of doing things. Be open to failures, which mostly become periods of learning and developing.

Be able to open yourself up so you can receive the merits of your outcomes and your goals. Yes, and mostly be open to receiving more than is expected, and more than you can visualise. Be open and prepared to exceed your expectations and those of others.

ASPIRATIONS OF MY GRANDMA

During the period of learning to aspire, as my grandma would say, I have spent some time acknowledging various things my grandma has achieved. The things that she created in her life, neighbourhood and her communities. I realise that the more I learn, the more I would hear 'the sayings' revolve in my head. Sometimes I meet and share my findings with other individuals who have been influenced by 'what my grandma would say', who would also tend to respect her sayings.

When reflecting on things I have heard; the sayings and the phrases I have mentioned, I revisit some of the physical locations and influences of my grandma. I sometimes sense a fascination at the communities my grandma built through her work. I still find some uniqueness existed in the true giving of herself. Through her passions and her love, my grandma wanted to help build families and help them heal.

My grandma's main purpose seems to have been the drive to help serve others. Her interest and desire to heal the sick has shown me a huge sense of humbleness. I believe I inherited and developed her sense of compassionate behaviour. Today, as I focus on achieving, exceeding and aspiring, as my grandma would say, I think of and relate to the things that she's done. My grandma helped to build communities and influenced community leaders and younger people. She built and left behind her legacy.

My grandma's contribution to healing the sick displayed her humbleness in creating what seemed to be a home and an atmosphere of peace and calm. I too urge you to consider that which you are aspiring to be. Aspire to become, however, with some sense of compassion and love. When you focus on the thought of what you want to achieve, why not put yourself in a position where you can help the less fortunate.

You can commit to giving and serving others in the form of charities. It could also be in the form of acknowledgements. What about sharing yourself or some of your time? Have you considered volunteering at some points on your journey?

My grandma instilled in me what other leaders have displayed as they gain and achieve a higher level of wealth. As they exceed to greater levels of their expectations, they can give back, exponentially. More than most people would give and especially in monetary forms. As I aspire, I think of the idea of philanthropy and picture how I can give back to people, my environments and the community. As I aspire and exceed expectations in my success levels, I continue to give time and gratitude for the inspirations of my grandma.

EXCEED IN WISDOM

While it is great to gain and learn and build on your level of intelligence, it is not always what you know that is necessary. For you to aspire and exceed beyond your expectations, you need to have connections. My experiences have taught me that it's not always what you know. Think more in the sense of some collaborative work. I have recognised that in bringing groups of like-minded individuals together, this tends to create higher energy levels. The higher authority, and a higher knowledge base than what you as an individual could ever attain will be available within your circle of influence.

Who you know, will always be a factor that will be explored in your journeys. It is who you know that will expand and develop your wealth of knowledge, your authority and your influence. Your wisdom may be limited to the extent of what you know. What you have learnt, and what you can access at times may be different resources. Who you know will create a powerhouse, and it can contribute to the idea of masterminding. You can bring like-mindedness together. Bringing different expertise to focus on a similar vision and a similar outcome will generate that power. Your know-how can help model your idea of exceeding your levels of wisdom.

Exceeding your current status or state, requires that you be action orientated. By being action-orientated, you build on your wealth files (in your head). Your knowledge and your own levels of intelligence develops. By being an action taker, and as you take the necessary steps to learn, you will gain access to resources of your know-how. The people that generally influence you when brought together within the same network can create a powerhouse. Exciting and rewarding expectations that are beyond your own wisdom can be accomplished. You will exceed your wisdom.

ASPIRE TO BE SUCCESSFUL

Success in any form will include your level of wisdom growing, expanding, or changing. Whatever your aspirations, this is what you will become. It is your aspiration to be a new you and to enhance or improve that you set out on another journey. In aspiring to be successful, you will set goals, and you must act. You will set goals to form a basis for your journey and for where you want to be. You will act as you must move towards your endpoint, you must lean towards your target.

I made mention previously of tracking your progress; it is in you setting your goals and taking the necessary action that you can plot your journey. Whether it's step by step, or by other methods, you must do this, and consistently, while on your journey. In plotting and accessing your steps, this is where your aspiration to be becomes seemingly fruitful. Aspiring to be successful is working for you and on you. It is you becoming a brand new you. It is you becoming a more focused you.

As you aspire, you will search, you will look within yourself, and you will explore what thoughts you have. Your mindset will be more action-oriented. You will be more active. And as you act, track your progress. It is in this focused effort that you achieve your goals and become successful. Being successful may take the form of monetary value. It may simply be the feeling of happiness, to you. Positioning yourself to be of a different posture may be your thing. Either way, being successful is often a result of happiness.

You could be happy where you are today, right now! Remember that it is through your own processes, Through your aspirations and your visualisation. You can formulate that picture of your vision, of where you want to be. You could become successful within yourself. In fact, within your mind, you can create a path to how you want to feel.

Why not set your goals and actions. While plotting your journey and while tracking your progress, you can be accountable, as you achieve your goals. There is a sense of joy that is enveloped in this path. The action plan and journey must start from within you. Aspiring to be successful will begin when you create that vision within you.

EXCEED YOUR THINKING

I alluded previously to your way of thinking within your thought processes. I believe you will agree that as 24 hours is set in a day, then everyone should have an equal amount of time to act. It is within these 24 hours that you must journey, like everyone else. These hours are from the start of the day, to when you call it the end of your day's activities.

I often start my day with some thinking time, before I access my mobile phone and possibly any form of technology devices. I like to think of the first part of my day as a thinking and preparation time. I choose to start with a period of silence, a period, most times, for prayer or meditation. I like to take the time out to focus on my affirmations, and I remind myself of what I'm seeking and what I'm venturing out on. My top tasks are set as part of my daily routine.

How about you? What is your daily start routine like? Is it productive or energy focused?

At times, as I access my 'daily (morning) flow', I search within for my daily reminders. After my period of silence, of prayer or meditation, I like to think. I channel my focus by adding additional time to visualise, the shaping and setting of paths for the day. I look at points of where I want to be at particular segments throughout the day's activities. As I plan, I try to take the time to think and be in mental control of some of the activities. I will make notes of some actions throughout the day and how I'll take them and when.

Although you may not control time, it's in speaking your thoughts through the form of your affirmations that preps your actions. Through the forms of your daily 'flows,' you can be in control of your thoughts and look beyond. You can go ahead of yourself in forms of accessible thinking. Creating the right level of mindset and setting the tracks ahead of you to take your journey throughout my day.

Exceeding your thinking will require you to stop at different points. Consider refreshing and invigorating your energy levels. Whether it be a liquid that you take in, especially water, rejuvenate and revive. Refresh yourself to re-establish your thoughts. You can give your body a 'time-out' periodically. Give yourself a refreshing and reviving feeling. Keep your thoughts in line with your aspirations, and this will assist in you exceeding your thinking.

Notes

"What Is Holding You Back From Taking Action"

www.asmygrandmawouldsay.com

Printed in Great Britain
by Amazon